Wysokie-Mazowieckie; Memorial Book (Wysokie Mazowieckie, Poland)

Published in Tel Aviv 1975

Published by JewishGen

**An Affiliate of the Museum of Jewish Heritage—A Living Memorial to the Holocaust
New York**

The Wysokie-Mazowieckie; Memorial Book (Wysokie Mazowieckie, Poland)

Translation of: *Wysokie-Mazowieckie; sefer zikaron*

Published in Tel Aviv 1975

Original Book Edited by: I. Rubin – Wysikie-Mazowieckie Society
Project Coordinators: Sandy Levin, Ada Holtzman z"l
Layout and Name Indexing: Jonathan Wind
Cover Design: Rachel Kolokoff Hopper

Published by JewishGen, Inc.
An Affiliate of the Museum of Jewish Heritage
A Living Memorial to the Holocaust
36 Battery Place, New York, NY 10280

The mission of the JewishGen organization is to produce a translation of the original work, and we cannot verify the accuracy of statements or alter facts cited.

Printed in the United States of America by Lightning Source, Inc.

Library of Congress Control Number (LCCN): 2021938580

ISBN: 978-1-954176-14-0 (hard cover: 228 pages, alk. paper)

Cover Credits:

Front and back cover background photograph:
Lost in the Garden by Rachel Kolokoff Hopper.

Front cover illustration:
The old house of study, built at the end of the 18th century, page 11 (Original page 16).

Back cover background map:
Wysokie–Mazowieckie in the 17th–18th centuries, up to the dissolution of the Council of Four Lands (1764), page 8 (Original page 12).

Back cover photos top from left to right:
Rabbi Aharon Ya'akov Perlman (may God avenge his blood), page 85 (Original page 141)
Yo'irkeh, the water–carrier, page 66 (Original page 119)
Dr. Golda Zak (may God avenge her blood), page 118 (Original page 193)

Back cover photo bottom:
The new synagogue, page 20 (Original page 26)

Back cover words:
From the "Forward" by Dov Kaspi, page 6 (Original page 10).

JewishGen and the Yizkor Books in Print Project

This book has been published by the **Yizkor Books in Print Project**, as part of the **Yizkor Book Project** of JewishGen, Inc.

JewishGen, Inc. is a non-profit organization founded in 1987 as a resource for Jewish genealogy. Its website [www.jewishgen.org] serves as an international clearinghouse and resource center to assist individuals who are researching the history of their Jewish families and the places where they lived. JewishGen provides databases, facilitates discussion groups, and coordinates projects relating to Jewish genealogy and the history of the Jewish people. In 2003, JewishGen became an affiliate of the **Museum of Jewish Heritage—A Living Memorial to the Holocaust** in New York.

The **JewishGen Yizkor Book Project** was organized to make more widely known the existence of Yizkor (Memorial) Books written by survivors and former residents of various Jewish communities throughout the world. Later, volunteers connected to the different destroyed communities began cooperating to have these books translated from the original language—usually Hebrew or Yiddish—into English, thus enabling a wider audience to have access to the valuable information contained within them. As each chapter of these books was translated, it was posted on the JewishGen website and made available to the general public.

The **Yizkor Books in Print Project** began in 2011 as an initiative to print and publish Yizkor Books that had been fully translated, so that hard copies would be available for purchase by the descendants of these communities and also by scholars, universities, synagogues, libraries, and museums.

These Yizkor books have been produced almost entirely through the volunteer effort of researchers from around the world, assisted by donations from private individuals. The books are printed and sold at near cost, so as to make them as affordable as possible. Our goal is to make this important genre of Jewish literature and history available in English in book form, so that people can have the personal histories of their ancestral towns on their bookshelves for themselves and for their children and grandchildren.

A list of all published translated Yizkor Books in the project with prices and ordering information can be found at:
http://www.jewishgen.org/Yizkor/ybip.html

Lance Ackerfeld, Yizkor Book Project Manager
Joel Alpert, Yizkor-Book-in-Print Project Coordinator
Susan Rosin, Yizkor-Book-in-Print Project Associate Coordinator

This book is presented by the
Yizkor-Books-In-Print Project
Project Coordinator: Joel Alpert
Associate Project Coordinator: Susan Rosin

Part of the Yizkor Books Project of JewishGen. Inc.
Project Manager: Lance Ackerfeld

These books have been produced solely through efforts of volunteers
from around the world. The books are printed using the Print-on-Demand technology and sold at
near cost, to make them as affordable as possible.

Our goal is to make this intimate history of the destroyed Jewish shtetls
of Eastern Europe available in book form in English, so that people can
experience the near-personal histories of their ancestral town on their
bookshelves and those of their children and grandchildren.

All donations to the Yizkor Books Project, which translated the books,
are sincerely appreciated.

Please send donations to:

Yizkor Book Project
JewishGen, Inc.
36 Battery Place
New York, NY, 10280

JewishGen, Inc. is an affiliate of the
Museum of Jewish Heritage
A Living Memorial to the Holocaust

Notes to the Reader:

We apologize ahead of time for the poor quality of images in the book. Often these images had been scanned from the original Yizkor books which were of poor quality to begin with, being copies of old photographs. Each transfer results in loss of quality. We have done the best we could, given the original material and the resources and technology at hand. Even though images often appear of higher quality on computer screens, that does not transfer to high quality images in print. A reader can view the original scans on the web sites listed below.

Within the text the reader will note "{34}" standing ahead of a paragraph. This indicates that the material translated below was on page 34 of the original book. However, when a paragraph was split between two pages in the original book, the marker is placed in this book after the end of the paragraph for ease of reading.

Also please note that all references within the text of the book to page numbers, refer to the page numbers of the original Yizkor Book.

The original book can be seen online at the New York Public Library site:

https://digitalcollections.nypl.org/items/34361f80-28af-0133-42bf-58d385a7b928

or at the Yiddish Book Center web site:

https://www.yiddishbookcenter.org/collections/yizkor-books/yzk-nybc314105/rubin-yosef-visoke-mazovyetsk-yizker-bukh

In order to obtain a list of all Shoah victims from Wysokie-Mazowieckie, the reader should access the Yad Vashem web site listed below; one can also search for specific family names using family name option. These lists are continually updated by Yad Vashem, so it is worthwhile to periodically search these lists.

There is much valuable information available on this web site, including the Pages of Testimony, etc.
http://yvng.yadvashem.org

A list of this book and all books available in the Yizkor-Book-In-Print Project along with prices is available at:
http://www.jewishgen.org/Yizkor/ybip.html

Geopolitical Information:

Wysokie-Mazowieckie, Poland is located at 52°55' N 22°31' E and 79 miles NE of Warszawa

	Town	District	Province	Country
Before WWI (c. 1900):	Wysokie Mazowieckie	Mazowieckie	Łomża	Russian Empire
Between the wars (c. 1930):	Wysokie Mazowieckie	Wysokie Mazowieckie	Białystok	Poland
After WWII (c. 1950):	Wysokie Mazowieckie			Poland
Today (c. 2000):	Wysokie Mazowieckie			Poland

Alternate names for the town:
Wysokie Mazowieckie [Pol], Visoka-Mazovietzk [Yid], Visoki [Yid],
Mazowieck [Pol, before 1866], Vysokie-Mazovietzkie [Rus],
Visoke Mazovyetsk

Nearby Jewish Communities:

Jabłonka 11 km WNW

Sokoły 14 km ENE

Wyszonki Kościelne 18 km SSE

Czyżew-Osada 19 km SW

Zambrów 19 km WNW

Rutki 21 km NNW

Łapy 25 km ENE

Andrzejewo 25 km WSW

Gać 26 km NW

Zawady 27 km NNE

Ciechanowiec 28 km S

Szumowo 29 km W

Suraż 29 km E

Brańsk 30 km SE

Nur 31 km SSW

Zaręby Kościelne 32 km SW

Wizna 33 km NNW

Tykocin 36 km NNE

Śniadowo 37 km WNW

Sterdyń 40 km SSW

Choroszcz 41 km NE

Piątnica 41 km NW

Kosewo 41 km W

Łomża 41 km NW

Małkinia Górna 42 km SW

Kosów Lacki 43 km SW

Jedwabne 43 km NNW

Ostrów Mazowiecka 43 km WSW

Prostyń 45 km SW

Boćki 47 km SE

Trzcianne 48 km NNE

Białystok 49 km ENE

Bielsk Podlaski 49 km ESE

Jewish Population: 1,910 (in 1900)

Map of Poland with **Wysokie-Mazowieckie**

Original Book Cover Page

ויסוקה־מזוביצק

ספר זכרון

הוצאת אירגון יוצאי ויסוקה־מזוביצק בישראל
תשל״ה — 1975

Translation of Previous Page

Wysokie – Mazowieckie

Memorial Book

Published by the former residents of Wysokie-Mazowieckie in Israel

5735 - 1975

TABLE OF CONTENTS

Jewish Personalities

The Holocaust

Testimonies

**The Martyrs List of the Holy Communities of
Wysokie Mazowiecki and Jablonka
May God Revenge Their Blood**

The English Part

Wysokie-Mazowieckie: Memorial Book

(Wysokie Mazowieckie, Poland)

52°55' / 22°31'

Translation of:

Wysokie-Mazowieckie; sefer zikaron

Edited by: I. Rubin – Wysikie-Mazowieckie Society

Published in Tel Aviv 1975 (H, Y, E)

———

Translation Project Coordinators:

<u>Sandy Levin</u>

Ada Holtzman z"l

Our sincere appreciation to Mrs. Yaffa Rosenberg of the Wysockie Mazowiecki organization, for permission to put this material on the JewishGen web site.

This is a translation from: *Wysokie-Mazowieckie; sefer zikaron.* Wysokie-Mazowieckie; Memorial Book
ed. I. Rubin, Tel Aviv, Wysikie-Mazowieckie Society, 1975 (H, Y, E)

Note: The original book can be seen online at the NY Public Library site: <u>Wysokie-Mazowieckie</u>

Please contribute to our translation fund to further the translations of other Yizkor Books.

JewishGen's <u>Translation Fund Donation Form</u> provides a secure way to make donations, either on-line or by mail, to help continue this project. Donations to JewishGen are tax-deductible for U.S. citizens.

ויסוקה מאזאוויעצק

ספר זכרון

[Page 8]

Foreword[1]

by D.K.

Translated by Yael Chaver

We debated for a long time:

How should we express the searing pain while preserving for eternity our holy dear ones and the community of our town, which had existed for centuries, and was completely destroyed by the foul Nazis, and their helpers, the cursed Poles?

We planted one thousand trees to honor them in the Forest of the Martyrs; we put up a memorial plaque in the Chamber of the Holocaust; but we knew that it was not enough.[2] These are only metaphors and symbols, and cannot describe the horrors endured by the Jews of our town. Such a description can be found in the memorial book, which recounts the history of our town as well as the culture typical of Jewish communities in Poland, and the particular features of the Wysokie–Mazowieckie community.

When we began to put our plan into motion, we encountered many difficulties, in collecting materials and gathering the financial means necessary for publication. The many considerations and efforts involved in these preparations – which took almost ten years – finally culminated in this result. True, the book is modest and short. We could not present detailed descriptions of many events as well as figures who left an impression on the town thanks to their talents and good deeds.

In addition to the limited financial means at our disposal, we had imposed another constraint on ourselves: we decided to describe only public and social events, and as few individuals as possible. We did this in order to prevent arguments and complaints on the part of our fellow townspeople, who might have been offended by the non–inclusion of their loved ones in the book (as has been the case in memorial books by survivors of other communities).

Nonetheless, the effort has been worthwhile, even though only several episodes have been included. First and foremost, the description of Holocaust events as set down by the Bialystok center for documentation, and as recounted by the following survivors:

[Page 10]

Peysekh Segal (may his memory be for a blessing), Leyma Plishka, Yaffa Rozenberg, Leya Zlotolow, Shlomo Vaynberg, and Avrom Hirshfeld. The List of Martyrs in this book is extremely important for the memorialization process.

The chapters on the life of our community before World War II, along with the images and the descriptions of a few typical characters and groups of community activists, combine to complement the last section–that of the tragic end and obliteration of our community.

* * *

Let this book be a modest monument and true witness to our sorrow and grief over the Jewish community of Wysokie–Mazowieckie, which was wiped from the face of the world so gruesomely.

––––––––

Translator's Footnotes:

1. This section is translated from Hebrew.
2. The Forest of Martyrs, on the western outskirts of Jerusalem, was planted as a memorial to those who died in the Holocaust. It contains six million trees, symbolizing the six million Jews who perished at the hands of the Nazis in World War II. The Chamber of the Holocaust, a small museum on Mount Zion in Jerusalem, was established in 1948, and was Israel's first Holocaust museum.

––––––––

[Page 9]

Foreword[1]

by D.K.

Translated by Yael Chaver

We debated for a long time:

How should we express our burning pain, and preserve for eternity the memory of our dear martyrs, and of the community of Wysokie, which existed for hundreds of years and was wiped out so gruesomely by the foul Nazis and the Poles, their cursed helpers?

We planted a grove in their memory, in the "Forest of the Martyrs"; but felt that it was not enough. These are only signs and symbols, which fall short of presenting a picture of the horrors and ghosts of the terrible fate that befell the Jews of our town. A *Yizkor Book*, however, can depict a partial picture of the events; such a book can recount the history of our community, the features that were typical of most Jewish communities in Poland, as well as the qualities specific to the Jewish community of Wysokie–Mazowieckie.

When we began realizing our plan for the *Yizkor Book*, we encountered serious difficulties – both in gathering the materials and in collecting the financial means for publishing the project.

Our doubts and efforts concerning publication of the book lasted for almost ten years, until we finally succeeded in creating the book that we had aimed at. True, the book is modest, and it lacks many details of important events and interesting figures who lived and were active in Wysokie, and left their mark of their talent and good deeds on the town.

Besides being limited by our small budget –which rendered the publication of the book difficult –we consciously limited ourselves by deciding to describe only important social and community events, and mention very few individuals, so as to avoid arguments and complaints by townspeople whose families and loved ones were not mentioned.

On the other hand, even the publication of a few chapters on Jewish life in Wysokie was worth the effort. Above all, describing the events of the great destruction, as provided through the Bialystok center for documentation, and setting down the memories of people who lived through the horrible period and survived it: Peysekh Segal (may his memory be for a blessing), Leyma Plishka, Yaffa Rozenberg, Leya Zlotolov, Shloyme Vaynberg, and Avrom Hirshfeld. Of special importance for their memorialization is the list of martyrs from our town in this book.

[Page 10]

The chapters on Jewish life in Wysokie before World War II, accompanied by pictures of typical characters, and community activists, present an authentic image of Jewish Wysokie, and complete the last section of the book: the scroll of the tragic, terrible, murder of our community.

* * *

Let this book be a modest monument and a true witness to the pain and sorrow that fill us whenever we recall the Jewish community of Wysokie–Mazowieckie, which was so horribly wiped off the face of the earth.

Book committee:

Dov Kaspi (Srebrovitsh), Moyshe Zak, Yisro'el Inbari (Burshteyn), Shloyme Reshef (Hirshfeld), Mikha'el Avigad (Ubanevitsh).

Translator's Footnote:

1. This section is translated from Yiddish.

[Page 11 - Yiddish] [Page 16 - Yiddish]

Notes on the History of Wysokie–Mazowieckie
(from its beginnings to the end of the 19th century)

Translated by Yael Chaver

Wysokie–Mazowieckie, near the Brok River, seven kilometers from the Szepietowo–Bialystok–Warsaw railway station, is one of the oldest settlements in Mazovia Province, Poland. It is mentioned as a settlement as early as the first half of the 13th century (in 1239). On the recommendation of Prince Aleksander, it was founded in 1494 by Hinczow as an urban settlement.[1] In 1503, it received privileges and rights as a city from King Aleksander, according to the Magdeburg rights of Germany. These rights were reconfirmed by kings Zygmunt III and Stanisław August. In the early 16th century, the town became the property of the Princes Radziwill, and belonged to the Princes of Nieswierz in 1582–1670. It was destroyed in the wars with the Swedes, in the mid–17th century. Following the third Polish partition (1795), it was annexed to Prussia. In 1807, it became part of the new Duchy of Warsaw and in 1815, following Napoleon's defeat, part of the Russian–controlled Kingdom of Poland. In 1866, it became a provincial capital.

* * *

There is no information on the beginnings of the Jewish community in the town. It is first mentioned in the records of the Council of the Four Lands, three centuries ago, in connection with taxes that were imposed on them.[2] A document of 1725 refers to the Jewish community of Wysokie–Mazowieckie directly, and recounts a quarrel between the Jewish communities of Węgrów and Ciechanowiec concerning which of them had authority over the Wysokie–Mazowieckie community. According to the document below, Wysokie–Mazowieckie was under the authority of Węgrów at the time; the leaders of the Ciechanowiec community disputed that authority. The dispute came before the Council of the Four Lands. The judges were Rabbi Yehoshua Levi and Rabbi Berish Segal, of Krakow, and representatives of the Ciechanowiec and Węgrów communities were present. As neither of the parties could prove their claim, the decision was that the Jewish community of Wysokie–Mazowieckie should be under the authority of neither.

The Verdict[3]

"In the matter of a legal dispute between the leaders of the Ciechanowiec and the Węgrów communities, concerning Wysokie, and as the leaders of the Ciechanowiec community claim that Wysokie is under their authority, they appeal to the leaders of the Council of the Four Lands, may God, their redeemeer, preserve them.

[Page 12]

Wysokie–Mazowieckie in the 17th–18th centuries, up to the dissolution of the Council of Four Lands (1764)

[Page 13]

"We, the undersigned, sit in judgment in order to determine who is in the right, and have brought both parties here to present their arguments in person. They have not exhibited their rights to us, saying that they do not possess the documents.

"Therefore, based on our judgment that all the claims of these parties are entirely oral, and as the parties have left, we have decided to postpone the trial until after the fair at Międzyrzec in the winter of 1725–1726. In the meantime, taxes collected for the royal treasury, on September 29, 1727, shall be paid in the following way: each community shall pay half of the poll tax imposed on it. When the trial resumes, we shall notify the parties to appear with their rights. Neither of them will have authority over the other on any legal matter. Only the two undersigned people shall have authority over them. The poll tax for this year totals 120 Polish crowns. Thus, 60 crowns must be paid by the leaders of the community of Węgrów, and 60 crowns each by the leaders of Węgrów and Ciechanowiec.

"We set this forth, and both sides agree to be bound by it and to make no changes, God forbid.

On the fourth day of Sukkot [September 24], 1725

Signed by Yehoshua HaLevi of Krakow (currently located here) of Ciechanowiec, member of the Council of the Four Lands.

and by Berish Segal of Węgrów ."

The trial was held in Sterpin (known as Asterdin by the Jews) near Ciechanowiec.[4]

(See *Historishe Shriftn*, vol. 2, published by YIVO, the article by Dr. Mahler; and *Pinkas Va'ad Arba Ha'aratsot*, by Professor Yisra'el Heilprin.)

* * *

Apparently, the issue of authority over Wysokie–Mazowieckie by one of the large provincial communities was not resolved by the verdict of the Council of the Four Lands. Forty years later, the Polish census of 1764 lists Wysokie–Mazowieckie as a semi–autonomous community. The census was overseen by a local committee, consisting of a "deputy leader" (deputizing for the community leader), the local rabbi and the manager, besides an "inspector" and a Polish noble assigned by the authorities. The fact that the town had a leader, a monthly leader as well as a deputy, a rabbi, and a manager, is evidence that the Jewish community was well–organized by then. However, it was small, and turned to the provincial town of Ciechanowiec for approval. Oddly, the Wysokie–Mazowieckie community was under the authority of Ciechanowiec, which was relatively distant, rather than under

[Page 14]

that of Tykocin, the oldest Jewish community in Mazovia province.

(The document about the 1765 census appears in the chapter "The History of Wysokie–Mazowieckie" (in Yiddish) in *Hebreish–Yidishe dokumentn fun di folkstseylungen in poyln*, by Dr. Raphael Mahler.)

* * *

A century later, in the second half of the 19th century, there were 600 Jewish families in Wysokie–Mazowieckie. A report in *HaTsfira* of July 1, 1879, states that the town's house of study was old and very dilapidated, and barely accommodated all the attendants.[5] (There was also a wooden synagogue, which burned down in one of the conflagrations that were common in the towns of Poland and Lithuania – most structures in these towns were wooden–and was never rebuilt.) It was apparently in such poor shape that the local police had issued an order prohibiting its use for prayer. The heads of the community decided to raise money from the residents and also sold seats, in order to construct a new house of study that would be fitting for a community of 600 people. In the meantime, however, the community leaders had quarreled, and the house of study was not built. The *Ha–Tsfira* report from Wysokie–Mazowieckie is presented below:

Wysokie–Mazowieckie (Łomża Province)

"The town includes six hundred Jewish families, but there was only one house of study, which was old, and dilapidated and unsound due to its age. It was also too small for the number of attendants. Finally, last summer [1878], the police issued an order prohibiting prayer in the structure, as it was too dangerous. When the townspeople saw that the doors had been barred, they collected contributions, and also sold seats, to facilitate a proper new structure; they made all the preparations. However, in the meantime, a quarrel broke out between the leaders of the community; therefore, their initiative flagged, and they withdrew from the building project. This is a sin against God and the people of Israel, because the provincial governor, Mr. Antonow, was pleased to contribute 150 rubles towards the construction of God's house; the leaders are to blame for its not being built, and that is a disgrace."

HaTsfira, July 1, 1879.

* * *

As in all the towns of Poland and Lithuania, the Jews of Wysokie made their living as storekeepers and artisans. Few were wealthy or well–off, with the exception of the Frumkin family, which owned an estate near the town. The Frumkins were one of the richest and most prestigious families in Lithuania and Belorussia. One branch of the family had settled in Grodno, and owned an estate in Wysokie. The family provided a livelihood for many Jews, as well as being itself very generous. Especially noteworthy in this respect was Mrs. Rivka Frumkin (wife of Eliyahu Frumkin), who was very generous and charitable. Mrs. Rivka Frumkin died on March 11, 1895. A eulogy of March 11, 1895, in *HaMelits*,[6] includes the following description: "... and in her home town of Wysokie–Mazowieckie, the poor are inconsolable, as she was like a mother to orphans, like a sister aiding widows and ill people who had survived the cholera epidemic that affected the town last year. She also prevailed upon her husband to open a food kitchen, where about 150 people received free food daily for about five months, until the epidemic ceased. This generous woman also took care of the last survivors and provided them with charity. "She opened her arms to the poor and extended her hands to the needy, near and far."[7]

[Page 15]

The Frumkin family left Wysokie–Mazowieckie many years before World War Two.[8]

[Page 16]

The old house of study, built at the end of the 18th century)

Translator's Footnotes:

1. I was unable to identify Hinczow.
2. The Council was the central body of Jewish authority in Poland from the second half of the 16th century to 1764.
3. This text is in the style of rabbinical legal documents of the time; I have presented its substance and attempted to preserve some of the original flavor.
4. I was not able to identify the location of Sterpin and Asterdin.
5. *Ha–Tsfira* was a pioneering Hebrew newspaper published in Poland in 1862 and in 1874–1931.
6. *HaMelits* was the first Hebrew newspaper in the Russian empire. It was founded as a weekly in 1860, appeared as a daily starting in 1886, and continued intermittent publication until 1903.
7. This sentence is a paraphrase of Proverbs 31:20.
8. The remainder of p. 16 as well as pp. 17, 18, and the first part of p. 19, have not been translated, as they duplicate the material on pp. 9–15, except for the figures. All the figure captions are included in this translation.

[Page 19 - Yiddish] [Page 31 - Hebrew]

Our Town in 1905–1918

by Dov Kaspi, Ramat Gan

Translated by Yael Chaver

This article recounts the town where I was born and grew up, and which I left in 1918, when I joined *He–Chalutz* in Lithuania, en route to the Land of Israel.[1]

The 1905 Revolution

The first event that impressed itself on me as a small child, and left a lasting effect, was the 1905 revolution. Social and political events caused upheavals in the enormous Russian empire. Galvanized by the revolution, the absolute monarchical regime made lavish promises to grant the peoples of Russia freedom and democracy and form a parliament (Duma) elected by the people. At the same time, the authorities suppressed the revolution brutally, and caused much bloodshed. In order to divert the masses, the tyrannical regime directly encouraged pogroms against Jews, carried out by unruly Cossack troops, and did so indirectly – by inciting the Russian Orthodox masses to abuse the Jews and rob their property. "Beat the Jews and save Russia" was the slogan under which the Black Hundreds led the inflamed masses to take revenge for "Great Russia" on its most dangerous "enemy" – the Jews.[2]

The 1905 revolution and its after–effects did not skip over our small town, which was set in its ways. Its monotonous life was quiet. However, in order to provide background for the events that took place in my home-town, I would like to describe its Jewish population and the groups that comprised it.

The Jewish population of Wysokie–Mazowieckie consisted of three more–or–less distinct groups: a) merchants; b) craftsmen; c) laborers, mainly apprentices, who learned their trade from the craftsmen they apprenticed with, and hoped to become independent craftsmen themselves once they became proficient.

[Page 20]

The laborers (or apprentices) copied the actions of workers in the large cities, and especially in nearby Bialystok, where there was a large number of laborers, mostly textile workers. Shifts of older workers came by daily to stop the apprentices' work if they exceeded eight hours. There were also monitoring shifts during strikes. The rebels also carried out "expropriations," by imposing tax quotas on the rich merchants (there were no real bourgeois in Wysokie, except for Frumkin, the landowner) for the benefit of the striking workers. Those who did not pay the tax voluntarily was punished by tactics of intimidation and terror.

Especially vivid in my memory are the tactics used against my grandfather, Simkha Kaplan (may his memory be for a blessing). He had a large store, where his daughters and sons–in–law worked. When he was unwilling to pay the tax, they used the fact that my uncle and aunt, Simkha Zak, and Rashka (may their memory be for a blessing) were about to get married. They ruined all the clothes of the family–the silk dresses of the women, and the satin clothing of the men, by pouring sulfuric acid over them while the bride and groom were being led to the khuppa ceremony in the square near the synagogue. That did not satisfy them – one night, a large stone was thrown through the window of my grandfather's house. Miraculously, no one was hurt; but my grandfather was so upset that he became ill, and did not recover until his death.

The Robbery of the State Bank

The most remarkable event was certainly the famous robbery of the Russian State Bank, the "Kaznachiestvo," by members of the Polish Socialist Party (P.P.S.), headed by Joseph Pilsudski–later the liberator of Poland from Russian authority, and who led Poland until his death in 1936.

Wysokie was the provincial capital, and housed the institutions of the provincial authority, including the State Russian Bank, which served the entire province. Among its other functions, this bank contained the salary money for thousands of government clerks throughout the province. At the end of each month, a large sum of money was brought to the bank for salary payments the next day. The bank was guarded by a small number of policemen, armed with pistols, with one stood at the bank's entrance. The guard was maintained around the clock, with changing shifts. The guard unit was reinforced by a company of about 100 soldiers (*rota*) that was housed outside town, with a bell connecting the barracks with the bank, in case of robbery. The company would be replaced every month by a different company, sent from the military base at Zembrów.

The change of guard unit took place as follows: the company that had completed its task left the place on the last day of the month, and the replacement company arrived the next morning. Members of the Polish Socialist Party utilized that interim period. One such night, forty men came, armed with rifles and explosives, cut the telephone lines, took the guards' weapons and handcuffed them. The operator of the bank's safe was then forced to hand over the keys; they emptied out all the contents of the safe: bills as well as gold and silver coins. They even took the copper *kopeks*.[3] The booty was loaded on to a few carts that had been forcibly expropriated from their owners (the owners were later compensated lavishly), and the robbers fled in different directions, to towns and villages nearby. Policemen from Wysokie and Zembrów pursued them; about ten of them were shot and killed during the chase. None of the robbers was injured.

[Page 21]

A few days later, the P.P.S. sent the Russian authorities a formal receipt for the money taken (after all, they did not consider it a robbery, but a revolutionary act supporting the liberation of the Polish people). As is well known, it was Josef Pilsudski who initiated, planned, and carried out the operation.

Obviously, the residents of Wysokie did not sleep at all that night. The revolutionary robbers warned them not to leave their houses during the night. The residents actually did stay awake all night and did not set foot outside, for fear of their lives. No one was injured, except for one young man, Noakh Visotshek, who reported that he had taken a pistol and rushed to save a family of friends, who lived above the bank. He was shot in the leg, and returned home wounded.

The robbers forced the cart–driver, Yosef Lifshits (may his memory be for a blessing), who immigrated to the Land of Israel after World War One, and died there, to drive the sacks of coins to a nearby village. The sacks were then loaded onto another cart, and the robbers fled.

The daring robbery, which was organized and executed out successfully, left a strong impression on all of Poland, as well as on other parts of the Russian empire. The residents of our town, who witnessed the audacious, violent robbery, were greatly affected by the event.

* * *

I have titled this chapter "Our Town in 1905–1918." However, the chapter should actually be divided in two sections, 1905–1914, and 1914–1918.

What was the town like in the decade of 1905–1914? I will try to describe it, based on my memory.

Like most towns in Poland and Lithuania, Wysokie–Mazowieckie was stagnating. Life was peaceful, and focused on two topics: making a living, and leading a rigorously observant life. Relations with the outside world were limited to merchant travel to the large cities of Bialystok and Warsaw, to buy merchandise, and to Łomża, the provincial capital, for dealings with the authorities. The Hasids in our town would travel to their rabbis' "courts," and the young men who wanted to become scholars went to study in *yeshivas*; first to the Łomża *yeshiva*, and then to the great *yeshivas* of Lithuania (Slobodka, Mir, and Radin) as well as to Lida, where they could also study secular subjects.[4]

[Page 22]

A Peaceful Life

The peasants in the vicinity were the main source of livelihood for the Jews of the town. Many Jews had shops around the "market" – the town's main square – and along several nearby streets. However, Jewish commerce was not limited to shopkeeping. There were merchants who dealt in timber, grain, and animals (horses, cows, geese, and the like); these traded with the landowners. They sent the goods they acquired to the large cities of Bialystok and Warsaw, and some even exported goods to eastern Prussia. The other field of enterprise was craftsmanship. The Jews in our town were tailors, hatters, cobblers, metal–workers, smiths, carpenters, ironworkers, glaziers, construction workers, and watchmakers. Some of them had shops in which they sold their wares.

The House of Study

The main business days were Monday and Friday, when farmers would throng to the town to sell their produce as well as purchase goods they needed, such as oil, kerosene, fabrics, tools, and housewares. They also bought objects such as hats, boots, shoes, and metal wares. Business was most lively during the "fair" days (occurring several times a year), when large numbers of farmers and merchants from the nearby and more distant vicinity congregated in the large "market" square. The square became filled with dozens of stalls, which sometimes collapsed under the weight of the goods they brought.

As a provincial capital, Wysokie enjoyed many customers; many people from the surrounding towns and villages needed the services of the government offices located there.

[Page 23]

These included the provincial offices, the court, the census bureau, and the state bank. The army draft office was also in Wysokie, where draftees from the entire province were instructed to appear. Call–up day was once a year. On that day, the town buzzed with hundreds of draftees – termed *rekruts*– and the parents and other family members who accompanied them. The young men (non–Jews) who were found to be fit for service spent the time between approval by the draft board and entrance into basic training camp by rioting throughout the town (knowing that they would not be punished); their rowdiness was primarily directed at the Jews, but they terrorized the entire town.

The draft office gave rise to another "source of livelihood", which was no great credit to our town. These were the fixers (*makhers*), who had connections with members of the draft board, and bribed them to let off draftees. The fixers, who were very competitive, informed on each other to the authorities. Obviously, this was not considered an honorable profession, and our town became "renowned" as "Wysokie *makhers*." However, many towns were given nicknames. For example, the neighboring town of Zambrów was called "Zambrow gangs," after the gangs that traded in stolen horses there; Tykocin was termed "Tykocin snobs," as it was the oldest town in the region. As is well known, Tykocin is ancient; the the records of the Council of the Four Lands state "Bialystok, near Tykocin." Of course, that was before Bialystok became a large city. Yet the residents of Tykocin remained proud of their lineage, although the town remained small.

Luckily, our town did not suffer from conflagrations, although most of its buildings were constructed of wood. This was not the case with nearby towns such as Zembrow and Czyżew, in which major fires occasionally broke out and burned down dozens, even hundreds, of buildings. As is well known, the fires served as time markers in many towns: "so and so many years after the first fire," ..." the second fire," etc. These towns changed their appearance after the fires, as many stone buildings were then constructed (especially in Zembrow). Wysokie, though, was an exception, as there were hardly any fires there. According to local legend, the town had been saved from fire thanks to the blessing of the old rabbi, the *tsaddik*, that it not be ruined by fire. When I was a child, I remember people coming on pilgrimage to his tomb in the old cemetery, near the synagogue. The small wooden houses were passed down from one generation to the next. Over time, brick buildings began to be constructed.. Especially imposing was the large structure of the provincial offices in the center of the "market," with a row of shops nearby. Imposing, privately owned, stone buildings could also be seen on other streets.

* * *

The Jewish landowner Frumkin had special status in our town, with his grand castle, brick buildings, and offices, at the end of "Courtyard Street." Mr. Frumkin himself did not mix with the residents of Wysokie. The heads and leaders of the Jewish community, along with Polish landowners and high officials, were invited only to important family occasions.

[Page 24]

At the end of the first decade and the beginning of the second decade of the 20th century, extremist Polish nationalists announced a boycott of Jewish commerce in Poland; for some reason, our town was one of the main fronts of this battle of the nationalists with the Jewish merchants.

As is noted elsewhere in this book (the correspondence of Netanel Zilbershteyn in *Ha–Tsfira*), the local priest who led the incitement organized his accomplices to carry out various operations against the Jewish merchants. Let me add that the anti–Semitic campaign was accompanied by some violence, and even the murder of Jews. Among them was my uncle, Shoul Kaplan (may his memory be for a blessing), who was shot in the neck while traveling from the nearby Shepetewo train station. His attacker was not arrested or brought to court.

Education in Our Town

During the period covered here, many young children studied in the only educational establishment available in Jewish neighborhood, the *kheyder*.[5] Our town had many *kheyders* devoted exclusively to religious studies(for boys only; girls did not attend them, but studied with tutors how to read the prayer book and a Yiddish translation of the Torah). The youngest boys learned to read Hebrew, and older boys read the Torah with Rashi's commentaries; the oldest boys older studied the Talmud.[6] In theory, the *kheyder* students were supposed to gain secular knowledge in the state school (the *szkole*), but in actual fact the Jewish students turned up there once or twice a year, when the state's Ministry of Education inspector visited.

At one point, the governor of the province was about to force the girls to attend the state school, and the community leaders opposed this edict. Their slogan was "*nie żylajem szkołes*" ("we don't want schools"). The decree was canceled. At the time, secular studies could only be done with the teacher Bogatyn, who had a short Russian beard. He arrived in our town from one of the cities in Russia. Along with his sons, who had studied there in *gymnaziya*, he disseminated secular education in our town.[7] Bogatyn and his sons opened a private school for Russian, mathematics, and othr subjects. His wife started a stationery store and sold books as well.

As noted, there were many *kheyders* in Wysokie, each at a different level. The first *kheyder*, or the lowest level, was for 3–year–old boys. Shilem was the *melamed*.[8] He was a nearsighted old man, with a white beard. Unlike other *melameds*, the students did not come to his house; rather, he taught them in their own homes. He used a pointed branch to indicate the letters, and the student would repeat after him until he learned to recognize the entire alphabet. He taught the children to read the prayerbook without teaching them the meaning of the words.

[Page 25]

The second–level *kheyder*, which boys started at age 4, was run by Avigdor, the amputee. He used to be a cart–driver before he lost his legs in an accident; with no means of livelihood, he decided to become a *melamed*. He would teach the first sections of Genesis. As he was legless, he would sit on the floor, with the students around him.

The third–level *kheyder*, for boys aged 5–6, was taught by Reb Khayim–Leyb the *melamed*[9]. He kept srict discipline in his *kheyder*. The students had to come at a specific time, and pay attention, understand the material, and learn it by heart. Reb Khayim–Leyb taught all the sections of the Torah, in Hebrew and in Yiddish translation. He wielded a strap, and enjoyed beating the bare buttocks of any boy who didn't know the lesson by heart, or misbehaved.

The next level was for boys aged 7–8, taught by Reb Mates (Matityahu) Rozin, who later emigrated to Israel, was the sexton of a synagogue in Tel Aviv, and died at a ripe old age. Boys there studied Talmud ("a page of the Gemara").[10] Reb Mates had a pleasant voice, and served as a volunteer cantor, especially in the Ger synagogue during the High Holy Days.[11] He was a polite, agreeable person, whom students liked, and therefore learned his material willingly. He taught other biblical material (mainly the Former Prophets) on Saturday afternoons.[12]

The fifth–level *kheyder*, for 9–10–year–olds, was run by Reb Mendl Berman. Reb Mendl was imposing in appearance, and a scholar who had to apply his knowledge to earn his livelihood.[13]He taught mainly Talmud, with all its questions and intense critical analyses and argumentation, sharpening the students' wits and logic.

The topmost level in town was for 11–12–year–olds, who were taught by Reb Velvl Kapusta, a *misnaged* (all the other teachers were Hasidim).[14] He was a scholar, with broad knowledge and a sharp analytical mind. His *kheyder* was mostly attended by students who intended to continue their studies in *yeshivas*. Unlike the other teachers, who ran their schools in their own homes, Reb Velvl taught in the small synagogue near the House of Study. His aim was to prepare the students for *yeshiva* study. Besides to these schools, the town also maintained a *talmud-toyre* for students whose families could not afford tuition.[15]

The *yeshivas* – beginning with the Łomża *yeshiva* and continuing with the great *yeshivas* of Lithuania – were the institutions of higher Jewish education, which prepared rabbis and teachers of Jewish religious law. Most of the students from our town did not use their education for making a living, but studied the Torah for its own sake. The *yeshiva* of Lida offered secular studies as well. The other *yeshivas* were exclusively dedicated to the study of the Talmud and its commentaries. Secular studies, including literature, were strictly forbidden. The prohibition was especially observed in the *yeshivas* that followed the *mussar* tradition.[16]

[Page 26]

Yet in spite of all the bans, the young students of the *yeshivas* were attracted to Hebrew literature and adopted the idea of the revival of Hebrew and the resettlement of the Land of Israel. *Yeshiva* students from Wysokie brought the message of modern Hebrew literature back to town, and disseminated it among our young people.[17]

This was also the time when the large daily Yiddish newspapers *Der Moment* and *Haynt* began to appear in Warsaw.[18] Thanks to them, many young people became familiar with Yiddish literature, and acquainted themselves with secular education as well.

The new synagogue

Political Parties

During the decade 1905–1915, there were no real political parties in our town. However, the ideological movements adopted by the Yiddish and Hebrew newspapers had their sympathizers. The only Zionist in the town was Reb Ya'akov Ratski (may his memory be for a blessing), who made sure that there was a contribution bowl for the Jewish National Fund among all the other bowls in the synagogue, every year on the eve of Yom Kippur.[19] This was no small task, as the synagogue managers opposed the Zionist bowl. But Reb Ya'akov Ratski fought for the rights of Zionist settlement in Palestine, even in the synagogue. He also disseminated the Zionist shekel, and earned the nickname "the shekel merchant."[20]

[Page 27]

Hasidim and *Misnagdim*

Almost every Jew in Wysokie was either a Hasid or a *Misnaged.* The *Misnagdim* were the majority, and prayed in the synagogue and the House of

Study. The hasidim prayed in the *shtibls*(small synagogues), each of which drew the followers of a particular Hasidic leader. The largest *shtibl* was that of the Ger Hasidim, which was located in a building on the Hinter Gas, near the river. The other *shtibls* used rented apartments. The most important of these were the Hasidim of Aleksander and of Vurke.[21]

Hasidim and *Misnagdim* had different world views and habits, but usually refrained from inciting disputes. However, wherever the community had to select a rabbi, ritual slaughterer, or other religious functionary, the differences between the factions rose to the surface, leading to much controversy in the town. The town rabbi, Rabbi Aharon Ya'akov Perlman (may his memory be for a blessing) was a patriarchal figure, a great scholar, and a pleasant person. He was a *Misnaged* and prayed in the House of Study. Thanks to his personality, he often decided in favor of the *Misnagdim*.

In addition to these centers of Hasidim and *Misnagdim*, our town also included a prayer group of young men and *yeshiva* students, called *Tif'eret Bakhurim*, which gathered for prayer only on Saturdays and holidays. They were not particularly observant, but "one must pray," as the writer Y. L. Peretz noted; as they did not feel comfortable in any of the other synagogues, they established their own congregation.[22] It should be noted, in their favor, that many of them volunteered to teach the *talmud toyre* students how to write in Hebrew and Yiddish, as well as arithmetic and other subjects.

During World War I, 1914–1918

The war years did not cause much disruption in our town. However, it was a time of major changes, which affected the town's future development. The changes began when the town was liberated from the tyrannical czarist regime, which hampered the Jews in all fields of life.

The retreat of the Russian army from east Prussia, and the town's occupation by the German army, were the start of a difficult period. As is well–known, the retreating Russian army was instructed to leave "scorched earth" behind it. The Cossacks, who were the last to leave, started to burn the buildings so as to destroy the town. The community leadership sent a delegation, headed by Rabbi Aharon Ya'akov Perlman, to the Cossacks' commander, begging for mercy and to leave the town intact; they even tried to bribe him handsomely. However, he did not respond to their plea, rejected the bribe, and fires broke out at the edges of town, at the Makom market square (in which Poles lived), and in the Hoyfishe street, where the post office was located.

I remember Cossacks bursting into my parents' shop and demanding kerosene in order to set the buildings on fire. My father (may his memory be for a blessing) claimed that there was no kerosene in the store, but the Cossacks did not believe him. They searched and found several barrels of kerosene in the warehouse. One of the Cossacks drew his sword and attacked Father; but my brother Yosef (may his memory be for a blessing) sprang towards the attacker, embraced him, and said, "Leave the old man alone. Come with me, and I'll help you take the kerosene." At that very moment, the

Germans entered the town, and the Cossacks fled before they had the chance to set fire to the town center, with its Jewish residents. Three or four buildings in the Hoyfishe street burned down, and a similar number – in the market area. It was in this way that the town was saved and survived intact. Life resumed its normal course a few days later. During World War I, under the regime of Kaiser Wilhelm, the Germans did not harm the Jewish population, and even granted them rights that they had been denied under Czarist rule. This was done in order to gain their sympathy and the sympathy of Jews all over the world – above all, of the large Jewish community in America. Very shortly afterwards, military rule was replaced by civilian authority. The German officials, who were mostly middle–aged, treated the Jews with tolerance and even formed friendships with the Jewish families they had dealings with.

[Page 28]

It is worth noting that public and social activity among Jews, which was officially prohibited under the Russian regime, flourished during the German occupation.

The Ark of the Torah in the New Synagogue

[Page 29]

Zionist activities were permitted, as well as secular cultural activities. Under the Czarist regime, such work had been extremely limited. Young Jews, anxious for education, thrived under the German authorities, who did not intervene in internal Jewish life; they began to develop various cultural and public enterprises.

The first project was the establishment of a public library. The initiators and main movers, who also constituted the first library committee, were Shlomo Zarembski, Ya'akov Litvak, Ayzik Levinski, Berish Serebrovitsh (Dov Kaspi), Moshe Kaplan, and the devoted, industrious librarian, Przebar. Once the library was established, education–starved Jewish young people had a path to Yiddish and Hebrew literature, as well as to world literature in translation. The library committee did not limit itself to a rich supply of books, but also invited lecturers and writers from Warsaw to speak, and organized debates by locals on various literary topics.

After the prohibition of Zionist activity was rescinded, Zionist organizations developed in the town in order to spread the idea of a national movement among the young people, as well as among other segments of the Jewish population. The first was a branch of Tze'irei Tziyon.[23] The first activists were Tzvi Galishinski (chairman), Moshe Kaplan, Sarah Burshteyn (now Sarah Tuvia, living in Israel), Benaya Tomkivitsh (now a lawyer in Israel), Yisra'el Brener, Ribko the teacher, and Moshe Tomkivitsh. The organization had a large clubhouse (next to the home of the Ya'akobi family), where it carried out many activities aimed at disseminating the Zionist ideal and intensifying it. Their practical activity consisted of collecting contributions for the Jewish National Fund, selling the Zionist *shekel*, organizing cultural evenings with nationalistic content, and the like. One of the most impressive events was the annual gathering on the twentieth day of Tammuz, the anniversary of Herzl's death; this event included varied activities.[24] Zionist awareness became so widespread that a rally was held in the synagogue for the first time. The house of study, which was used mainly by opponents of Zionism, did not invite Zionist activists. Especially vivid in my memory are the speeches of young Benaya Tomkivitsh, who spoke with great fervor, in a strong voice that echoed in the large hall with its high ceilings, and inspired his listeners.

Some time later, a branch of the Po'alei Zion party was founded in Wysokie, at the initiative of Khayim Bar–Nakhum –Skutshendek (may his memory be for a blessing).[25] It was active among young people, where it spread socialist Zionism, and the idea of emigration to the Land of Israel, after agricultural training.

At that time, a branch of the Maccabi sports organization also opened in the town. The first coach was a German soldier named Meichsner, who had served in the German occupation army. He took on this job, not because he loved Jews, but because he enjoyed leading young people in drills. We would meet several times a week on a lot outside town, and spend many hours drilling, marching, and running. At the end of each meeting we would form two teams and play handball. Each team did its best to win.

[Page 30]

That was the first sports club in our town; it was active for a number of years, and its members were the best children in town. After sports clubs were organized in neighboring towns, a convention of all the sports clubs in the region was organized in Zembrów; each club's delegation carried its own Zionist–sports flag.

Education also took a turn for the better under the German occupation. The traditional *kheyder* was no longer predominant; modern, progressive educational institutions developed alongside it. Reb Nokhem Skutshendek, who had come from Jedwabne on the German border (the town was burned down in the war), founded a "modern *kheyder*." The Vysochek family organized a school for boys and girls; classes were taught in Yiddish.

David Ya'akobi (may his memory be for a blessing) organized an amateur theater group consisting of young men and women, and trained them for theater performance. This theater mounted plays by Ya'akov Gordin, Avraham Goldfaden, and others.[26] The troupe was almost entirely run by Ya'akobi. He was the director, set constructor, and the star of the productions. This first theater in our town existed for many years. David Ya'akobi was also active in public affairs, and was for years the deputy chairman of the city council; he was later elected council chairman. One of his major roles was in the *Tarbut* organization.[27] He was also a photographer, and most of the images in this book are his work, as well as that of his student Sonia Kolodny (may she live long), who now lives in Israel and is continuing her work.

Thus, the years of German occupation during World War One signaled an important improvement in the social, cultural, and political lives of the Jewish community in Wysokie. These trends continued later in independent Poland.

Dluga Street – the long street

Translator's Footnotes:

1. *He–Chalutz* was a Jewish youth movement that trained young people for agricultural settlement in the Land of Israel.
2. The Black Hundreds was a reactionary, monarchist and ultra–nationalist movement in Russia in the early 20th century.
3. The *kopek* was the smallest denomination of the currency.
4. Hasidism began as a spiritual revival movement in what is now Ukraine, in the 18th century. A Hasidic community is organized in a sect known as a "court," led by a *Rebbe* (also known as a tsaddik – righteous man). Hasidim were categorized by their leaders' place of residence. Akin to his spiritual status, the *Rebbe* is the supreme figure of authority, as well as the administrative head of the community. Sects often possess their own synagogues, study halls and internal charity mechanisms, and ones sufficiently large also maintain entire educational systems. A *yeshiva* is an advanced school of studying Talmud and rabbinical subjects. The Slobodka *yeshiva* was founded in the Slobodka suburb of Kaunas in about 1881. The Mir *yeshiva* was founded in 1815 in the Belarusian town of Mir. The Radin *yeshiva* was founded in the town of Radun (Belarus) in 1869. All three *yeshivas* continue to exist in various locations. Lida is in Belarus.
5. The *kheyder* is a religious elementary school for boys.
6. Rashi (the acronym for Rabbi Shlomo Yitzkhaki, 1040 – 110), today generally known by the acronym *Rashi* (see below), was a medieval French rabbi and author of comprehensive commentaries on the Talmud and on the Hebrew Bible. His commentaries remain extremely popular and are widely studied to this day.
7. The *gymnaziya* was a secular secondary school.
8. *Melamed* is the term for a *kheyder* teacher.
9. Reb is widely used as an honorific for men; not all Kheyder teachers were rabbis.
10. Gemara is the Aramaic term for the Talmud.
11. The Ger Hasidic group, founded in Poland in the mid–19th century, is one of the largest and most influential groups. Its center today is in Israel.
12. Ultra–Orthodox education does not usually include portions of the Bible other than the Torah. The biblical books of Joshua, Judges, Samuel, and Kings are known as the Former Prophets.
13. In this traditional culture, scholarship is pursued for its own sake, and, ideally, should not be used for mundane purposes such as earning a living.
14. The ideological split between Hasidim and their opponents (termed *misnagdim*, from the Hebrew root for "opposition") was very strong.
15. *Talmud–toyre* students received an elementary education in Hebrew, the Torah, the Talmud, and some religious law.
16. The *mussar* movement, which developed in the 19th–century Lithuanian Jewish community, focused on education towards an ethical life.
17. European Jews used Hebrew exclusively as a sacred language up to the mid–19th century, when secularists began using it for everyday purposes. The secularist use of Hebrew became identified with Zionism, which aspired to resettle the Jews in the tradition homeland.
18. *Der Moment* (1910–1929) appeared in Warsaw, as did *Haynt* (1906–1939).
19. The Jewish National Fund was founded in 1901 to buy and develop land in Ottoman Palestine for Jewish settlement
20. Purchase of the Zionist Shekel gave the purchaser the right to vote for delegates to the Zionist congresses.
21. The Aleksander Hasidic group originated in the city of Aleksandrow Lodzki, Poland, in the early 19th century. The Vurke group was founded in the early 19th century in the town of Warka, Poland.

22. Yitzkhak Leyb Peretz (1852–1915) was a major European Jewish writer and cultural figure, whose works were very popular.
23. Tze'irei Tziyon was founded in Russian (1903) as a Zionist, Socialism–oriented movement of young Jews who supported emigration to the Land of Israel, physical labor, and the Hebrew language.
24. Theodor Herzl (1860–1904) is considered the founder of political Zionism. The Jewish month of Tammuz typically corresponds to late June or early July
25. Poa'lei Zion was a Zionist socialist political party in Poland, Russia, and Ukraine, founded in 1906.
26. Ya'akov Gordin (1853–1909) and Avraham Goldfaden (1840–1908) were major figures of the early Yiddish theater.
27. *Tarbut* was a widespread network of secular, Hebrew–language schools in Poland, Romania, and Lithuania, during the interwar period.

[Page 48]

The Polish Boycott of Jewish Commerce in Wysockie–Mazowieckie

by Natanel Zilberstein

Translated by Yael Chaver

In the early 20th century, the real authorities in the Polish provinces of the Russian Empire were the National Democrats, headed by Dmowski.[1] The party was extremely anti–Semitic; one of its goals was to deprive Polish Jews of their economic status. As the Jews made their livelihood by commerce and artisanship, this anti–Semitic party declared an economic boycott of Jews in 1909–1910, with the slogan "Don't buy from Jews, buy only from Poles." The boycott grew more severe in 1912, before the elections to the Fourth Duma. Wysockie–Mazowieckie was one of the places in which the National Democrats carried out virulent agitation against the Jews; this was headed by the local priest. Below is the report by Netanel Zilbershteyn, published in *HaTsfira* on January 31, 1913.

HaTsfira, January 31, 1913.

Mazowieckie, Łomża County.

Relations between Jews and Christians have been good, until now. The peasant would come to town and sell his produce, then go to the Jew's shop to buy whatever he needed. Although there are two Christian–owned shops in town, the peasants prefer the Jewish–owned shops–for the simple reason that the prices there are cheaper. However, matters deteriorated after the Warsaw Polish press began to announce the boycott. There is some unrest: the peasants say that whenever they gather in church, the priest forbids them to buy from the Jewish shops; and his words are obeyed. The priest would sometimes appear at the municipal offices, when peasants had business there, and disparage the Jews. The nobles in the region were also not idle. They gathered twice in our town and founded a society to fight against the Jews; they even established a savings and loan bank (which the Jews did not have). They decided to open a joint shop for peasants – the nobles themselves stopped doing business with the Jewish shops long ago – and are also planning to open a large wholesale warehouse... All of this did not lead the Jews to take any defensive steps. But the latest incident was such that the Jews could not stay silent. The town's municipality called to close the shops and taverns every Sunday. Naturally, the Christians immediately agreed, as they did not own any shops or taverns; the few Jews who were present refused to sign this resolution. Several days later, several Jews came to the municipality on business. The town secretary, along with the town head, demanded that the Jews sign the resolution, and threatened them if they did not. Not knowing the content of the resolution, the Jews signed. In this manner, they entrapped four simple Jews, and thought they would be able to catch a few more signatures. Then they would inform the county head that the entire town wanted to see this done – though we Jews are the majority of the residents. The Jews found out about this, and were furious at the great fraud the Christians wanted to carry out against us. We sent two letters, one to the county head complaining about the priest who was inciting hatred between Jews and Christians, and the other to the commissioner of peasants, asking to annul their resolution to close shops and taverns on Sundays. We hope they will not be able to carry out their evil plan."

[Page 49]

Translator's Footnote:

1. Roman Dmowski (1864–1939) was the chief ideologue of the National Democracy right-wing nationalist political movement, one of whose characteristics was anti–Semitism. It was known by its initials ND as Endecja; its members were called Endeks.

––––––––

[Page 51]

Pogroms Against the Jews of Wysokie–Mazowieckie in 1920

Translated by Yael Chaver

The period of the Polish Republic began ominously for the three million Jews living there – the largest concentration of Jews in Europe after World War One. The liberated Poles celebrated their independence by carrying out pogroms against the Jews. The Jewish community of Wysokie–Mazowieckie received its share of the Poles' rampage (August 1920), and the Jewish delegates in the Polish Sejm (Grynbaum, Hirshhorn, and others) protested to the government and demanded that the pogromists be punished.

The protest of the Jewish delegates and the demand for punishment were expressed in the Polish–language newspaper *Kurier Poranny*, on August 26, 1920. The article appeared in Hebrew on October 17, 1920, in the Hebrew–language newspaper *HaTsfira* in Warsaw:

Demanding Justice for the Events of Wysokie–Mazowieckie

On August 26, 1920, the Prime Minister spoke with an assistant from *Kurier Poranny*, and praised the actions of the Jews of Wysokie–Mazowieckie (and Łomża). The *Kurier Warszawski* of September 3, 1920, reported that a local partisan force (with the participation of Jews) had been organized in Wysokie-Mazowieckie, and had expelled the Bolsheviks from the town two days before the Polish Army returned. Thirteen Jews died in this battle. As they retreated, the Bolsheviks took 230 Jews and two Poles with them. The Polish Army rescued them from the Bolsheviks, but took the chance to rob, beat, and torture the rescued Jews. The army also plundered and beat the Jewish residents of the town.

The events in Wysokie–Mazowieckie are clear evidence that the Jewish population was the victim of robbery, murder, and pogroms (compared with Łomża), not only where they were unjustly accused of treason, but also where they exhibited their patriotism by taking up weapons against the enemy and suffering casualties. To a certain extent, this attitude towards Jews is the result of criminal propaganda by individuals and groups. As long as the true perpetrators of the anti–Jewish pogroms are not punished, baseless accusations against the Jews will continue to spread unchecked and unpunished.

For all these reasons, the elements guilty of these pogroms should be brought to justice.

HaTsfira, No. 219, October 17, 1920.

———

[Page 53]

The First Zionist Emigrants to the Land of Israel

Translated by Yael Chaver

Two people from Wysokie were among the members of the Second Aliya.[1] The first was **Barukh Burshteyn** (may his memory be for a blessing). He was a native of the village of Piechoty, which was part of the Wysokie community. His family was well–to-do, and owned an estate and a shop. At age 17, he left his home and emigrated to the Land of Israel.[2] He worked as a laborer in the Jewish settlements. Once the Jewish Legion was formed, he joined it and served until it was disbanded at the end of World War One.[3] He was then one of the organizers and founders of *moshav* Ein–Hai (now Kfar–Malal), which was established in 1913, and abandoned during World War

One.[4] He then started a successful farm, and one variety of the Annona (Cherimoya) fruit bears his name. His son Yitzkhak was a founder of *moshav* Lakhish. Barukh Burshteyn died a few years ago, after a long life spent building, and defending, the Jewish community of the Land of Israel

Ahuva Ederman was the first woman from Wysokie to emigrate to the Land of Israel with the Second Aliya. She worked in the Central Cooperative office for a long period, and has only recently retired.

Immediately after World War One, when the borders between the new state of Poland and its neighboring states were opened, the first members of the Third Aliya left.[5] **Dov Kaspi** (Berish Srebrovitsh) was the first to go, at the end of 1918. He left his wealthy parents and moved to neighboring Lithuania, where the *HeHalutz* movement had already been organized and there were agricultural training facilities. He participated in establishing the *Akhdut* group.[6] When the group started doing agricultural work on a Jewish estate near the village of Werblin, his brother **Yeshayahu** (may his memory be for a blessing) and their cousin **Yosef Bauman** (**Banai**). The entire group left for the Land of Israel in 1919, and its members were among the first Zionist workers after World War One to labor in the Hadera forest as woodcutters and as agricultural laborers for the farm–owners.[7]

[Page 54]

Members of the *Akhdut* group of *HeHalutz* in Lithuania, preparing to go to the Land of Israel
Third in the middle row: Dov Kaspi
Bottom row, middle: Yeshayahu Kaspi; to his left Yosef Banai

After the riots of 1920 broke out in the country, and the Arab workers in Hadera attacked the town, the farmers vowed to employ Jewish workers exclusively.[8] Yeshayahu Kaspi (may his memory be for a blessing) was the chief shepherd of the town; his assistant was Moshe Soroka (may his memory be for a blessing), later the chief administrator of the Kupat Cholim health organization.

Dov Kaspi and two other *Akhdut* members postponed their emigration in order to continue their agricultural studies in a school in Germany, where they stayed for two years. They emigrated in 1921. Once all three family members were in the country, the group settled in Karkur. The "Karkur group" existed for five years, with the aim of settling there permanently. However, a shortage of available land and water, as well as disease (malaria, typhus, jaundice, etc.) caused the group to leave the site and disband.

[Page 55]

One of the first emigrants after World War One was Shamai Kolodny, who emigrated in 1920 and worked as a carpenter in Hadera; he later brought his entire family over. He was active in the tradesmen's union. Others who emigrated from Wysokie in the same wave were the Burshteyn brothers; they followed their brother Barukh (may his memory be for a blessing) who had emigrated with the Second Aliya. These, Avraham (may his memory be for a blessing) and Yehuda (long may he live) emigrated in the early 1920s and were among the founders of the city of Ramat Gan. During that time, their sister Sarah Tuvia–Burshteyn and her husband, the engineer David Tuvia (may his memory be for a blessing), who planned and built many structures in Ramat Gan and Tel Aviv, also emigrated.

————

Translator's Footnotes:

1. The Second Aliya (1904–1914) was an important and highly influential *aliyah* (wave of Zionist Jewish emigration to the Land of Israel), during which approximately 35,000 Jews immigrated into Ottoman–ruled Palestine.
2. I have used the literal translation of a traditional Hebrew term (*Erets–Israel*) for the ancestral homeland of the Jewish people.
3. The Jewish Legion (1917–1920) is an unofficial name used to refer to five battalions of Jewish volunteers (the 38th to the 42th) Battalions of the Royal Fusiliers in the British Army, fighting against the Ottoman Empire during World War I.
4. The *moshav* is a cooperative community of farmers.
5. The Third Aliya lasted from 1919 until 1923.
6. *Akhdut* was one of the Zionist youth groups that were training to emigrate to Palestine to become farmers.
7. The city of Hadera was founded by proto–Zionist Jewish settlers in 1891.
8. The 1920 riots of local Arabs against Jewish residents and British law–enforcement (April 1920), mainly in and around the Old City of Jerusalem, caused the deaths of five Jews and four Arabs; several hundreds were injured.

————

[Page 56]

The Beginnings of the Mizrachi Movement in Wysokie–Mazowieckie

Translated by Yael Chaver

The newspaper *Dos Yidishe Folk* of August 9, 1917, describes the founding of a branch of the Mizrachi in Wysokie.[1] The article follows below, in translation:

"On Thursday, the 19th day of Elul, a branch of the Mizrachi movement was established in our town, by Lovers of Zion, religiously observant Jews, and young adherents of the Enlightenment; its purpose was to bring together Jews from various backgrounds in a religiously observant Zionist organization.[2] At the founding meeting, the speakers were Mr. Srebovitsh of Łomża, who spoke about the development of Zionism and the Mizrachi movement, and Rabbi Broyde, who described "historic moments" since the founding of the world Mizrachi movement. A committee was elected, with the following members: Rabbi Gershon Broyde, Mr. Pesakh Skubranek, and Dov–Ber Slyepovich. Ya'akov Ratski and David Bermzon represented the Lovers of Zion, and the young people were represented by A. Visotski (Secretary) and Feivel Zarembski.[3]

[Page 57]

* * *

HaTsfira of November 15, 1917, recounts: "During the Sukkot festival, the members of the Mizrachi held a grand celebration of the Water Drawing Ceremony.[4] The town rabbi spoke, and 100 rubles were collected to clothe the children of the poor. A public assembly took place on Simchat Torah, with several speakers, who drew many enthusiasts to join the Mizrachi movement.[5]

* * *

Contributions to the Jewish National Fund also increased as a result of religiously observant Jews' joining the Mizrachi. During the six months between the first day of Nissan (March 24) 1917 and the first day of Tishri (September 21) 1917, 83 marks and 50 pfennigs were collected for the Jewish National Fund in Wysokie.

(From a report in *HaTsfira*)

————————

Translator's Footnotes:

1. This may be the Yiddish–language weekly published in New York in the years 1909–1917.

2. The Lovers of Zion movement consisted of organizations founded in Russia in response to the late 19th–century pogroms and are considered proto–Zionists. They aimed to promote Jewish immigration to the Land of Israel and advance Jewish settlement there.
3. As the last names are not vocalized, they are transliterated.
4. A celebration connected with the ceremonies held at the Jewish Temple.
5. Simchat Torah ("The Joy of the Torah"), immediately following the Sukkot festival, celebrates and marks the conclusion of the annual cycle of public *Torah* readings, and the beginning of a new cycle.

———

Between the Two World Wars

Translated by Yael Chaver

Economic Conditions

As in all the towns of Poland, the economy of the Jewish population in Wysokie was based on commerce and artisanship. The Jews bought agricultural produce from the peasants in the environs and sold them manufactured goods. As the nearest railroad station was in Szepietowo, seven kilometers away, many Jews made a living by cart–driving and carrying loads. The goods ordered from Bialystok and Warsaw had to be unloaded and reloaded at the Szepietowo and Wysokie stations and delivered to the shopkeepers. There were many workshops in town, all small. The owner himself worked and employed no more than two or three apprentices. Before World War One, Wysokie had a factory; it was destroyed during the war and never rebuilt. The sole reminder of that factory was a well that was used by the townspeople. Thirty or forty percent of the Jews in Wysokie were poor and undernourished; many of the shopkeepers also had trouble making a living.

Relations with the Christian population were not especially friendly, even though the commercial ties were strong. Although the peasants sold most of their agricultural produce to Jews, while shopkeepers and artisans supplied the peasants with clothing, kitchen utensils, tools, and other products, a barrier of alienation steadily rose between them.

[Page 58]

Wysokie was occupied by Germans throughout almost the entire four years of World War One. Members of the Polish Legions, who organized at the onset of the war to exploit the battle between the international powers in order to liberate Poland from foreign rule, hid in the Masowian forests, and molested the Jews in the meantime. Two Jews from Wysokie, returning from nearby villages where they had bought eggs and chickens, were attacked and robbed by Legionnaires. When the German authorities found out, they punished the Legionnaire robbers. Seeking revenge, the Poles attacked the two Jews, killing one and wounding the other.

After the retreat of the German forces, at the end of World War One, the town was in an unusual situation. The Polish forces were unable to control the town and establish stable authority, as the Soviet Red Army was nearby. Having no other choice, the Jews organized a temporary authority until matters became clear. There were ongoing skirmishes between the Poles and the Bolsheviks, and the town changed hands. In one case, after seven Communist soldiers were killed by the Poles, the Bolsheviks retaliated by setting fire to the town. The town would probably have burned down, were it not for the Polish soldiers who arrived and extinguished the conflagration. The Poles were eventually victorious, and the entire region became part of the renewed Polish Republic.

Jewish children after World War One, supported by the JDC

[Page 59]

The Jews were neutral in the war between the Poles and the Bosheviks, though some circles of Jewish youth supported the Bolsheviks. Among them were members of the *Po'alei Tziyon* party, which had been founded shortly before; they cooperated with the Soviet regime that took over the town.[1] When one of the Soviet leaders was killed, and the authorities held a commemorative event, members of *Po'alei Tziyon* participated. The man was buried in the center of town. Once Polish rule was established, his grave was opened and the remains discarded.

After the Bolsheviks had finally retreated, some *Po'alei Tziyon* members joined them. Only a few actually moved to Russia. Several were able to emigrate to the Land of Israel, and others emigrated to Argentina and other countries of Latin America. However, most of the young people remained in the town and attempted to become part of the economy of the new, nationalistic Poland. All these efforts failed. Whereas the older generation was able to adjust to the new conditions and struggled for survival, the young people faced the implacable difficulties of the economic situation and the extreme anti–Jewish policies of the Polish authorities throughout the twenty years' existence of an independent Poland. Conditions were so bad throughout the 1930s that a considerable part of the Jewish population was totally dependent on frequent aid from relatives in America.

It is worth noting that, despite the general distress of most of the Jewish population, there were no beggars in Wysokie. The occasional beggars seen in the town came from elsewhere.

The constant deterioration of economic conditions intensified competitions between the shopkeepers, sometimes to the point of grotesqueness: a shopkeeper standing outside his shop waiting for customers would snatch a bottle of kerosene from a Polish passer–by in order to force him into the shop.

The difficult daily struggle for subsistence led to the realization that establishing common financial institutions, based on mutual aid, would make life easier. This was basis for founding a cooperative bank; the founders were both shopkeepers and artisans. As the majority were artisans, the shopkeepers accused the board of preferential treatment towards the artisans. Once mutual trust had been eroded, the shopkeepers split up the institution and created a bank of their own. Wysokie then had two credit institutions: the artisans' cooperative bank and the shopkeepers' bank. The town also had a traditional mutual–aid fund, which granted small, short–term, interest–free loans to shopkeepers and artisans. It was headed by Ya'akov Cohen.

Charity Societies and Aid Institutions

Wysokie, like all the cities and towns of eastern Europe, had traditional charity institutions as well as more modern assistance organizations; the latter were established in the decades preceding World War One.

Among these institutions were the hostel for travelers, the poorhouse, societies to aid the sick, needy brides, etc. Several weeks before Passover, the community leaders collected money in the town to make sure that no one lacked matza and potatoes for the holiday. One year, Khayim–Meir Goldman collapsed and died while doing this sacred work. The Jews of Wysokie thought highly of the command to give charity anonymously to those in need who were embarrassed to ask openly. The leaders would collect money every Friday and give it secretly to the needy. Every Friday evening, after lighting the candles, the righteous woman Yehudit would visit all the homes in the town, gather challah, and give it those who could not afford to buy or make their own.

[Page 60]

The Jews of Wysokie had this fine custom: on market and large fair days, when many women were tending stalls and shops, the neighboring women took care of their children as long as the parents were busy making a living.

The damp climate and malnourishment that affected much of the population led to the spread of tuberculosis; the death rate among children was especially high. Thus, the hospital that the town Jews established was extremely important for public health. During the last years before World War Two, the town had government health service as well

A rally before the Sejm elections

[Page 61]

Of course, Wysokie had a burial society, which provided proper funerals and ensured maintenance of the cemetery.

In the 1920s, the traditional aid and charity societies were augmented by new expressions of mutual aid. Especially noteworthy was one project: young Jews organized supplies of books and learning materials to poor Jewish students in the state–run elementary school. The best students were assigned to help the weaker students with their homework. Students also collected food and clothing items every Thursday and gave them to the poor students as a Saturday gift.

Culture and Education

Wysokie was a town with an atmosphere of study. There were many people from well–establihsed families, as well as many scholars. Reb Yankl (Levi's son) taught the daily Talmud page in the small synagogue of the Ger hasidim. A Mishna society was also established, and the artisans studied a chapter of that work every afternoon at the House of Study, between the afternoon and evening prayers. This society was led by Reb Nakhman Tzemakh. Wysokie also had an Ein–Yaakov society, led by Reb Asher Faygenblum, who would recount the wonderful legends; they, too, met in the House of Study. Reb Yisra'el Leyb, the synagogue's caretaker, led the classes. Less learned folk joined the Psalms society. These were people who were busy making a living all week, and could devote time to spiritual matters only on Saturday afternoons. Reb Khone Abetshkes, their manager, would read the chapters out loud, and the group would repeat them verse for verse.[2] Reb Khone also took responsibility for keeping the Eternal Flame burning.

In addition to these "organized" societies, religious students would study together in small groups of two or three. As noted, learning played an important role in Wysokie. A talented scholar was more important than an unlearned rich man. The status of Reb Berl Brizman, the caretaker of the Ger synagogue, is a good example. He was a poor man who barely subsisted on an allowance.[3] However, he was a great scholar (it was said that he knew the entire Talmud by heart), and thus enjoyed high status in the town. He was respected by all, and was considered a great authority on many talmudic matters.

Some of the famous scholars of Wysokie were Reb Nakhman Tsemakh, Reb Gershon Broyde, Red Alter Zak, Reb Yankl Levis (Slodki), Reb David Kahanovitsh. Reb Eliyahu Rubinshteyn, and others. Also noteworthy was the righteous great rabbi Veller, who lived several generations ago. The following incident was told: a fire broke out in the town on Saturday, and the righteous man extinguished it with one wave of his handkerchief. He also blessed the town to escape conflagrations. The Jews of Wysokie were certain that their buildings –largely built of wood – were safe, thanks to this blessing.

[Page 62]

In fact, any fires that broke out affected only the Christian streets.
* * *

Until World War One, the *kheyder* dominated education in Wysokie.[4] Talmud students would go to study in Łomża and then go on to the famous yeshivas of Lithuania, such as those of Mir, Slobodka, Volozhin, Radin, etc. Adherents of the *Mussar* movement, founded by Rabbi Yisra'el of Salant, opened a yeshiva in Wysokie, with 70–80 students from Wysokie and the surroundings.[5] These students were supported by householders in Wysokie.

* * *

Modern education began in Wysokie during World War One. The fighting between the retreating Russian army and the advancing German army caused several towns near the German border to burn to the ground, and many Jews who were left homeless sought refuge in other places that were untouched by the ravages of war. This was how a refugee from Jedwabne, Reb Nakhum Skutshendek, arrived in Wysokie. Reb Nakhum was descended from a line of distinguished rabbis, and was a traditional scholar as well as a modern scholar. Although he was close to the Ger hasidim, he opened a modern *kheyder* in which modern spoken Hebrew, mathematics, and other general subjects were taught, in addition to religious subjects. After his death, his son Khayim–who was a superb pedagogue–headed the *kheyder*, expanding and improving on his father's work. The modern *kheyder* closed during the Bolshevik invasion.

A Talmud–Torah

In 1921, the Polish government instituted compulsory education for all children below 14. A special government school was created for the Jewish children, called *Shabasovka*, as it was closed on Saturdays. That was the only difference between the *Shabasovka* and the general school. Classes were taught in Polish, and the curriculum followed that of the general elementary school.

The *Shabasovka* existed until 1933, when classes began to be held on Saturdays as well; it then became a general school that was attended by Christian and Jewish children alike.

The first principal of the *Shabasovka* was Butlov, and was later replaced by Rozental, a teacher from Łódź, who was a gifted teacher and a fervent national Jew. He was interested in every child and visited their homes to better understand their needs. When there was no budget to open a seventh grade, he started an evening class for twelve girl graduates of sixth grade. He also attempted to start teaching Hebrew and Yiddish, but the school authorities stood in his way. He used the time earmarked for religious studies in the curriculum to teach Jewish history, mounted plays for the Hanuka festival which were performed in Yiddish as well as in Yiddish versions. Yankl Lev was the Hebrew teacher.

A *gymnaziya* existed in the town for two years; in the late 1930s, when Polish anti–Semitism became so strong that Jewish and Christian children could not study together, it became a business school. It was then that the Jews of Wysokie decided to establish a *Tarbut* school. Coincidentally, a dispute broke out at the Talmud–Torah. Although the latter was semi–progressive, it did not satisfy those young people who were members of Zionist youth movements. They demanded a modern Hebrew school, along the lines of *Tarbut*. These two events – the *Shabasovka*'s transformation into a general school, and the revolt of the young people – led to the establishment of a *Tarbut* school, which developed well and had seven grades. Its activity was not limited to educating young children; it also organized adult Hebrew lessons and joined the effort to spread Zionist ideas by cooperating with the Zionist youth movements. The *Tarbut* school had its own building, as well.

[Page 64]

Political Parties and the Youth Movements

A branch of Tze'iri–Tziyon was organized in Wysokie as early as during the German occupation of World War One. It carried out intensive Zionist activity. Shortly afterwards, the Skutshandek brothers opened a branch of Po'alei–Tziyon. Their major achievement was encouraging young Jews from well–to–do families to break free of the prevalent prejudice against physical work (considered beneath their dignity). Three bridges were then being constructed near Wysokie; Shamai Kolodny organized these young people to go and work on these bridges. The Po'alei–Tziyon work brigade also participated in the construction of the Jewish hospital. The members of both Zionist Labor parties organized rich cultural and educational activities, established a drama club, and had occasional festive evenings ("balls").

The first clash between Po'alei–Tziyon and conservative circles in the town occurred before the municipal elections in the new Poland. *Po'alei Tziyon* organized a mass political rally in the House of Study, where most of the congregation were artisans. When the richest man of the town, Shoulke Kaplan, found out, he rushed to scatter the crowd, brandishing his thick stick. When the crowd mounted a strong opposition, he marshalled the Hasids, who had unexpectedly come to pray the afternoon and evening prayers in the House of Study. There was great commotion, and the rally could not proceed as planned.

The Zionist youth movements that had reached their peak in eastern Europe during the 1920s and 1930s inspired the youth to develop and progress. In 1927, representatives of *HaShomer HaLe'umi* from Bialystok came to Wysokie and established a branch of the movement there. They were followed by *HaNo'ar HaTziyoni,* which became the largest youth movement in Wysokie.[6] *HaShomer HaLe'umi* was founded by Dr. Tsherniavski and Khayim Halperin of Bialystok, and Moshe Galishinski of Wysokie. This movement encouraged its members to study Hebrew, held talks on Zionist topics and carried out practical Zionist activity, predominantly for the Jewish National Fund. The Zionist parties and youth organizations established a "folk university," which offered weekly Friday night lectures on public issues, literature, and science.

Students of the government elementary school

[Page 65]

However, the primary aim of the Zionist youth groups and, to a large extent, the Zionist parties as well, was emigration to the Land of Israel and the training necessary to achieve this goal. Emigration actually started as early as 1919–20. The first to go were the brothers Dov (Berish) and Yeshaya Kaspi (Srebrovitsh) who, together with

Bauman, were trained in Germany and emigrated from there in 1919. The first to emigrate directly from Wysokie to the Land of Israel were Arieh Wiecha and Shraga Burak. They left Wysokie at the end of December 1925, and arrived in the Land of Israel in early January 1926.

The *HeHalutz* organization began its activity in Wysokie in the early 1920s, through the work of Khayim Slodki and Khayim Burshteyn.[7] The most important project was establishment of the training camp, which eventually served the entire area. *HeHalutz* ran a training farm in Wysokie, which eventually had to close for financial reasons. However, *HeHalutz* also helped many members to gain expertise in other areas besides agriculture. Arieh Wiecha learned carpentry thanks to his training there, and worked as a carpenter in the Land of Israel for over 40 years.

As the Zionist youth movements developed, their older members (over age 18) became very active, and many of them emigrated once they received immigration certificates from the British Mandate authorities. Some older members of Zionist parties were also able to emigrate. One of these was Eliyahu Grinshteyn, Chairman of the local Zionist organization, who was killed during Israel's War of Independence.

Wysokie was largely a Zionist town. The Zionist parties *Po'alei Tziyon*, *Tze'irei Tziyon*, and the General Zionists set the tone.

[Page 66]

A wedding in the town

The Zionist Revisionists, and their youth organization Betar, with about 30 members, also opened a branch in Wysokie. Another, semi–military, organization was *Brit HeHayal*.[8] The religiously observant circles were organized in the Mizrachi movement, which – regardless of its small size locally – had considerable influence over the Wysokie population. The Mizrachi members were very active in the Zionist funds (the Jewish National Fund and the Jewish Foundation Fund). Their head was the veteran Zionist Ya'akov Ratzki.

There were very few non–Zionist public organizations. The Bund had very few sympathizers.[9] Agudat–Yisra'el had limited influence, and that mainly among the Ger hasids; they were headed by Reb Shlomo Kiweiku. The Communist party was not very popular, either. It comprised a small number of members, who were active in secret. They did manage to organize a labor union, which mounted cultural activities.

* * **

The political and economic conditions of the Jews worsened by the day. Wysokie was one of the few places that underwent a pogrom in 1936 (described elsewhere in this book). Yet, in spite of the generally serious situation, public and cultural activities continued without interruption, until the tragic end, when most of the town's Jews were martyred, along with the overwhelming majority of the Jews of eastern Europe.

[Page 67]

Elections in Wysokie–Mazowieckie

Voting for the 19th Zionist Congress, 1935:

General Zionists ("On Guard")	92
General Zionists ("Time to Build")	10
Mizrachi, *Tze'irei He–Halutz HaMizrachi*	97
S. Z. and *Po'alei Tziyon Yamin*	173[10]

Voting for the 20th Zionist Congress (1937):

Mizrachi	97
Labor Bloc	173

(From Dos Naye Vort newspaper, July 30, 1937)[11]

Voting for the 21st Zionist Congress, 1939:

General Zionists	11
HaNo'ar HaTziyoni	207
Mizrachi	45
Yidnshtatspartey	2
Labor Bloc	192
Leftist *Po'alei Tziyon*	1

Results of voting for the town council, according to the new elections system (*Kurjas*) (June 1939)

OZON (ruling party)	5 delegates
Endecja	3 delegates
The Jewish party	3 delegates

———

Translator's Footnotes:

1. Po'alei Tziyon ("Workers of Zion") was a movement of Marxist–Zionist Jewish workers founded in various cities of Poland, Europe and the Russian Empire around the turn of the 20th century.
2. Many Jewish communities offer a daily regimen of learning the Talmud, in which each of the 2,711 pages are covered in sequence. The Mishna, comprising six books, is the first major written collection of the Jewish oral traditions. Ein Ya'akov is a compilation of all the stories, parables, and exegeses in the Talmud together with commentaries. Many communities practice the custom of reciting chapters of Psalms. The 150 chapters are grouped into seven portions, so that they can be completed every week, and into thirty portions, so that they can be completed every Jewish month. Some people recite Psalms according to the weekly cycle, while others follow the monthly cycle.
3. The source of this allowance is not mentioned.
4. Original note: For information about the different *kheyders* and their levels, see Dov Kaspi's article "Wysokie in 1905–1918".
5. The *Mussar* movement, which focused on ethics, education, and culture, developed in 19th–century Lithuania.
6. Zionist political movements often splintered and formed new groupings.
7. *HeHalutz* trained young people for agricultural settlement in the Land of Israel and became an umbrella organization of the pioneering Zionist youth movements.
8. The Revisionist Zionist movement, headed by Ze'ev Jabotinsky, supported territorialist maximalism and sought to settle in the full territory of the traditional Land of Israel. The *Brit HeHayal* group within Revisionism consisted of former members of the Polish army.

9. The Bund was a secular Jewish socialist movement.
10. The groups referred to in quotation marks and by initials were factions that splintered off from the main party. S. Z. was a Socialist–Zionist faction.
11. I was not able to identify this newspaper.

[Page 68]

Photographs

Translated by Yael Chaver

A group of Zionist pioneers in training

The Zionist Organization Committee

[Page 69]

A farewell party for Eliyahu Grinshteyn, about to leave for the Land of Israel

A Wysokje youth organization, celebrating Moshe Galishinski's emigration to the Land of Israel

[Page 70]

A group of *HaShomer HaLe'umi* members, chopping wood

The "Hashmona'im" group of *HaShomer HaLe'umi*

[Page 71]

Activists of the Jewish National Fund

The Kana'im group of HaSHomer HaLe'umi, marking the emigration of Aryeh Vrubel and Ya'akov Nitsevitch to the Land of Israel

[Page 84]

A Town that Has Everything

by Rabbi Simcha HaCohen Kaplan

Translated by Yael Chaver

"Lovely and pleasant during their lives, in their death they were not separated" (II Samuel 1, 23)

The town of Wysokie–Mazowieckie is very dear to my heart, as some of its residents were my relatives. Whenever I came to visit, I felt that all the residents were related to me–Grandmother and Grandfather lived on one street, my uncles and aunts on both my mother's and father's sides lived on another street, and all were notable citizens of the town. This is why I cannot –and do not want to – ignore my special connection with the town, in order to describe it impartially.

I must admit that I am certainly not objective towards the town, as I always considered it more handsome and generally better than the other towns of the region. As a child, I studied there, as did my entire family, and enjoyed the sense of holiness and purity there. The townspeople's struggle to exist and to make a living refined their spirit. Even the least educated resident was more spiritual, and strove for improvement more, than the educated non–Jews who lived in the town and its environs.

[Page 85]

There were great scholars in Wysokie. Even in that generation, when great rabbis and scholars served in the small towns, these "householders" were unusual in their fluency and intellectual ability. Each of them had brought considerable knowledge from the great *yeshivas* where he had studied; over time, each had further deepened his knowledge. These scholars did not use their education to make a living. They were traders, who sat along the prestigious east wall of the synagogue.[1] First of all, I must mention my uncle, Rabbi Gershon HaLevi Broide (may his memory be for a blessing), who was eventually appointed Rabbi and *Moreh–Tsedek* in Suwalki, though he lived in Wysokie for most of his life.[2] I would also like to mention a nearby neighbor to whom I was very close – the scholar and Ger *hasid*, Rabbi Ya'akov Levis Sladki (may his memory be for a blessing). Although he was not officially appointed rabbi in the town, he substituted for the rabbi if the latter was away, and was the de facto rabbi of the Ger *hasid im* in the town.[3]

There were many scholars in the town; even the shopkeepers and artisans would study some Talmud between the afternoon and evening prayers. Some of them were very astute, others were leaders of Polish hasidic groups. They included intellectuals – young people who had studied at universities abroad. Among them were some of my family members: Dr. Isser Ratski, and my cousins Dr. Sima Zakimovitch and Dr. Golda Zak (both had received M.D. degrees from the Prague university). They had deep religious and secular knowledge; Judaism was part of their personality, and they enriched the town and its environs.

The elderly rabbi of the community, Rabbi Aharon Yaakov Perelman (may his memory be for a blessing) was at the center of community life. He had studied at the Volozhin *yeshiva*, and was the town's Rabbi for over fifty years.[4] In addition to his eminence as a scholar and and legal authority, his brilliance, intelligence, and gifts as a leader, qualified him for the authority of the town rabbi; all the affairs of the town and its environs were decided by him. The surrounding towns of Shepetova, Dombrovka, Serdinice, Wysonek, and others were under his authority.[5]Good, modest Jews had lived in these towns for generations, and Rabbi Perlman took care of their needs.

There were schools, such as a *yeshiva* for young children, and a number of elementary religious schools. I remember the voices of sweet young children on the street leading downhill. I visited that street on Friday afternoons, in order to hear the melodious sounds of these young voices as they studied the weekly Torah portion. I well remember the regular tests in the kheyder, when my uncle, the knowledgeable and sharp–witted scholar Alter Zak, would come and administer the tests–as well as the gifts of money that the best students would receive.

All that is gone now. My heart aches for the town of Wysokie, with its great men and children, its old and young, its schoolboys and older youths, its wealthy and well–off, its famous and its modest, its *hasids* and men of action, its simple working class. I no longer have the strength to lament them.

[Page 86]

"Mourn as for an only son, most bitter lamentation" (from the Lamentations for Tish'a Be–Av).[6] "Mourn as for an only son" is interpreted as mourning for all the victims of the Holocaust. May their memory be blessed forever and ever, may their souls be bound up in the bundle of the living. "Blessed is he who comes, and waits, and sees the rising sun illuminate your dawns, in which your steadfast share the happiness of your lost youth, restored as it once was."

Translator's Footnotes:

1. The most important men of the community had seats at the eastern wall of the synagogue, nearest the Ark of the Torah.
2. *Moreh–Tsedek* is a legal scholar who makes a decision in cases of Jewish law where previous authorities are inconclusive. The town of Suwalki had a large and important Jewish community.
3. Ger Hasidism was founded in GÃ³ra Kalwaria, Poland, in the 19th century. It is one of the largest and most influential hasidic groups worldwide.
4. The prestigious Volozhin yeshiva was active in the 19th century and until the outbreak of World War Two, in the town of Valozhyn, Belarus.
5. I was not able to identify these place names.
6. The first quote in this paragraph is from Jeremiah 6, 26, and is part of the lamentations said on the ninth day of Av, the traditional date of the destruction of the Jewish temple in Jerusalem. The second quote is from a poem of longing for Zion by the great medieval Hebrew poet Yehuda HaLevi, also included in the lamentations for the Ninth of Av.

The Pogrom in Wysokie–Mazowieckie, 1936

Translated by Yael Chaver

It was Monday, September 14, 1936, three days before Rosh HaShana–the day of the weekly market. As usual, traders had come from Łomża, Bialystok, and other towns in the area, bringing goods to sell to the peasants from the region, who came to Wysokie to sell their produce and buy goods that they needed.

The tension was noticeable from the early morning on. Unsavory characters started appearing in the marketplace, harassing the shopkeepers, threatening them, and demanding that they not unload their wares. The traders ignored them and set up their wares in stalls. The "picketers" (guards) upset trade all day, inciting the peasants not to buy from the Jews.

Up until 3:00 p.m.–in other words, as long as the peasants were still selling their produce – things were more or less tolerable. However, after 3:00, disturbances began. The bullies overturned the stalls and damaged the goods; the stall owners, mostly women, were beaten up. At 4 p.m., a whistle signaled the next stage (apparently, overturning stalls, damaging goods, and beating women were the preparatory phase). Dozens of bullies, soon joined by hundreds of peasants, rushed the Jewish shops, beat and stabbed the shopkeepers, and plundered the wares. Not only the Jewish shops were attacked, but their homes as well. Stones hailed down on their windows, and countless panes were smashed. Attempts were also made to break into the homes. Once the pogrom began, many shopkeepers abandoned their shops and wares, and fled for their lives. Many goods were carried away, or damaged. Some Jews were seriously wounded and needed hospital care.

It is worth noting that throughout the duration of the pogrom (until past 6:00 that evening), the police took no steps to control the situation. According to a different version, the district governor, the local chief of police, and a number of policemen were on the street the entire time, who spoke with the bullies and tried to calm them down, but were unsuccessful.

[Page 87]

* * *

Once the pogrom was over, the leaders of the Wysokie community informed the Aid Committee of the Warsaw Jewish community, the Joint, and Senator Professor Moshe Shur of the calamity that had occurred.[1] Mr. Volkovitsh, the secretary of the Aid Committee, communicated twice with the heads of the Wysokie community, and immediately sent a special messenger to investigate and promise aid to those in need. Prof. Shur wrote to the Interior Ministry and reported the information he had received, with special emphasis on the local authority's lack of initiative to prevent the disaster and to control events after they began. He also demanded that the Ministry instruct the governor in Bialystok to take immediate steps so that similar episodes should not happen in the towns of Sokoły, Zembrów, and others. The Interior Ministry immediately contacted the Bialystok governor and ordered him to suppress any attempt at violence.

The Jewish Polish–language newspaper *Nasz Przegląd* was the first to send a special representative to Wysokie to report on the pogrom.[2] On September 19, 1936, the day after Rosh HaShana, a detailed report appeared in the newspaper; below is an extract from this report.

"… The closer we get to Wysokie–Mazowieckie, the more the catastrophe that has overtaken this unfortunate town is noticeable. Evidence of destruction is everywhere. It is impossible to make even a superficial estimate of the damage. Should we walk from house to house and count the number of broken windowpanes, demolished windows, smashed ovens, broken tools and instruments? There are no accurate numbers of injured people. About thirty wounded were transferred to Łomża, Warsaw, and Czyżew. Seven casualties are in Zembrów.

On Thursday, the first day of Rosh Hashana, the governor of Bialystok, Mr. Kortikos, visited Wysokie–Mazowieckie, and issued some urgent orders.[3]"

The newspaper's representative concludes his report as follows: "The mood in the city during the two days of Rosh HaShana was that of fear, doubt, and tears…"

* * *

The day after the pogrom Dr. Vaynberg of Bialystok came to examine the injured and make a report. His list includes 23 wounded, whom he examined in the community office. Their names are:

1. Yisakhar Zlotolow, aged 26, who had been standing in the market at a stall selling notions and blue dishes (kitchen wares?). The marauders beat his back and hands with sticks. He has back pain, and one hand is bandaged.
2. Yitzkhak Hertz, aged 30. He was hurrying to save his sister's wares at her stall. He was wounded on the forehead and nose. One side of his face is swollen.
3. David Ogorek, aged 21, a grain merchant. He was stabbed in the back with a knife.

[Page 88]

4. Nekhama Ederman, aged 65, a baked–goods seller. She was beaten with an iron bar to the head. her nose and one eye are swollen.
5. Khaye–Gitl Ribak, aged 76, a milk–deliverer. Her head was hit by a stone.
6. Batya Zlotolow, aged 17. She stood by a stall. She was hit in the eye.
7. Shlomo–David Briker, aged 41, a water–carrier. His head was hit by a stone.
8. David Kamenetzky, of Buczki. He was bruised, and his wares were discarded and scattered.
9. Binyamin Zlotolow, aged 25. He was wounded in the head.
10. Betzalel Malakh. The pogromists scattered ten bolts of white cloth that he owned, and he was bruised on the head.
11. Hirshl Blum, aged 68, a peddler. He was beaten on the head.

12. Esther–Gitl Butshian, aged 70, a dealer in second–hand white cloth. She was wounded by a stone. Her face is swollen.
13. Tzivia Shchingl, aged 20, a seamstress. She was beaten over her knees with a stick.
14. Batya Zlotolow, aged 28. Her hands were bruised.
15. Dina Shlyukhter, aged 38. Her hands were injured by a bowl.
16. Brayna Zlotolow, aged 48. She was beaten with a stick and has bruises all over her body.
17. Hirsh–Leyb Burak, aged 48, a bath–house attendant. He was injured in the head.
18. Sara Tsimbel, aged 35. Her hands were bruised.
19. Hirsh Karbet, aged 55, a tailor of ready–made clothes. He was bruised in the head by a stick.
20. Shmuel Tabak, aged 18, a yeshiva student who was helping his mother in a stall of manufactured goods. He was hit in the hand with a stick.
21. Hinda Yakovnitzer. She was standing near her house when a peasant driving by in his cart gave her a blow to the head.
22. Mordekhai Vrubel, aged 40, a water–carrier. He was bruised in the head.
23. Zelig Vongerka, aged 72, owner of a water mill outside the town. He was injured in both hands and is in serious condition. He was in his house when a hooligan burst in and wanted to beat him. The old man ran from the house to the stable. His attacker chased him with an iron bar. The old man begged him, "Don't kill me. Have I done anything to you?" The hooligan struck him in the head with the bar. Luckily, the old man was able to cover his head with both hands, and thus survived. The old man began to weep: "What have we come to? My mill has been serving the peasants for over twenty years. I have never offended anyone, and always lived peacefully with the peasants."

Besides the above–noted 23 injured, there are five more in Sokoły, Zembrów, and Łomża. All were at their stalls in the market. Their wares were robbed and damaged. The injured have returned to their homes.

The reporter for the Bialystok Yiddish newspaper *Undzer Lebn*, who came to Wysokie on the eve of Rosh HaShana, describes the general mood in the town, and presents some details (which we include here, somewhat abbreviated).[4] The reporter was accompanied by a few journalists and by Dr. Vaynberg, mentioned above.

[Page 89]

"The entire Bialystok region is infected with wild anti–Semitism. People ascribe this to the activity of the previous government representative, a member of the Endecja (the most reactionary and anti–Semitic political party in Poland).

... We pass the village of Jablonka. Our Jewish taxi–driver says that two Jewish families, who owned taverns, had lived there. As early as a few weeks ago, he saw the sign "Polska Restauracja" (Polish Restaurant) on the taverns. He was told that the peasants of Jablonka threatened the two Jews with setting their homes on fire if they did not leave the village.

The trip from Bialystok to Wysokie–Mazowieckie, over 50 kilometers, took slightly over an hour.

We enter the market, and the unusual conditions in the town are immediately evident. All the shops are closed, except two, which have signs "This is a Polish store." Groups of people are gathered and talking in various corners of the market.

We were surrounded by dozens of Jews the moment we exited the car. When we asked why the shops were closed, the community's representative replied that the Aid Committee's meeting had decided to close the shops until the county governor, Dr. Swiakewicz, promised that peace would be restored.[5]

As we look around, the most noticeable thing are the blank windows and the broken panes. The municipality lists 1600 broken windowpanes, 170 broken gates, three sewing machines, three smashed ovens, and damaged wares valued at thousands of złotys.

Community clerk Watnik leads Dr. Vaynberg into the reception room for examining those wounded.

The community headquarters is near the House of Study, whose windows were also broken. It consists of two rooms, recently remodeled, with new furniture and large pictures of national leaders on the walls. Vaynberg examines the wounded, notes their names, and the type of each individual injury. The headquarters soon fills with dozens of Jews with bandages, eye coverings, etc.

…We leave, to take a look at the town. Broken windows stretch as far as the eye can see. On one street, there is a single undamaged house among all those with broken panes. This is because it is the home of a Christian midwife. It seems that the hooligans carried out their outrages according to a clear plan. The windows were broken even in a dilapidated wooden house, considered the oldest building in town. The pogromists did not spare even the most miserable hovels. Many of the windows were broken by stones large enough to kill a person, had they struck one.

[Page 90]

We enter the home of a Jewish seamstress. The floor is littered with parts of a demolished sewing machine; the poor seamstress is standing and ironing the dresses she had already made. How will she earn a living now?

The Jews in the town tell us about the course of events. A few days before market day, the peddlers from the nearby towns asked whether attacks by hooligans were anticipated. The response was that the local authority had promised that order would be strictly kept and that the market day would be peaceful. And in fact, the police kept closer guard that day, and reinforcements were sent to Wysokie.

… We decide to visit the county governor, Dr. Swiakewicz. Inside the government building, we meet a Jewish delegation (including the rabbi) that had just emerged from the governor's office. The deputy mayor, the Jewish Ya'akobi, demanded that the authorities pay damages to the injured. The governor ordered the shops to be opened, and informed the delegation that all steps had been taken to ensure that such events would not recur. They also told us that, during their meeting, the governor had made serious accusations against the local police, which had apparently not changed their habits from before he was appointed governor. He also notified the delegation that the chief of the local police had been suspended from duty.

We are told that the governor will see us shortly, but the Bialystok district governor, Mr. Kortikos, suddenly appeared and went directly into Dr. Swiakewicz's office. This visit left a strong impression on the entire population; however, the interview with the press was canceled.

* * *

The day after Rosh HaShana, a Jewish delegation was seen by the deputy Bialystok district governor. This delegation included the head of the Bialystok community, Mr. Lifshits, the head of the Wysokie–Mazowieckie community, Mr. Bielski, and the community clerk, Mr. Watnik.

The delegation gave a detailed report of the pogrom, emphasizing several dramatic details that made a strong impression on the deputy governor, Mr. Grzobinak. He was especially shocked at hearing about the acts of the hooligans when they saw the 200 chickens that the Jews had bought from the peasants for the holiday. The chickens were locked in cages; the pogromists broke the cages open and strangled the chickens. He was also impressed by the report of the hooligans breaking into a house in which seven sisters lived and earned a living using a single sewing machine; the machine was smashed to bits.

The deputy governor promised the delegation that the authorities would prevent any future attempt at rioting and would suppress any acts of violence. He also asked the Jews of Wysokie to carry out a detailed survey of the events of that day, and present it to the district authorities.

As mentioned, the new Bialystok district governor, Mr. Kortikos, came to Wysokie, and was interested in what had happened. He made a detailed investigation, and ordered the arrest of several suspects who were the organizers and perpetrators of the attacks on the Jews. It emerged that some of the hooligans had come from other places; almost all of them were "Endek" activists.

[Page 91]

* * *

(The data about the pogrom in Wysokie–Mazowieckie are from the newspapers *Undzer Lebn* of Bialystok, *Haynt*, *Moment*, and *Nasz Przegląd*.)[6]

Telegram from the Writer Sholem Asch to the Jews of Wysokie

"I wish to express my deep sympathy with the catastrophe you have undergone, and send you good wishes for the New Year, in my own name and in that of millions of American Jews. I promise you that your sufferings are shared by the congregations of tens of thousands of synagogues where Jews are gathering during these holy days. Your torturers and enemies are our torturers and enemies as well. May this be some consolation to you."

The Jews of Wysokie responded to the great author by telegram through the Jewish Telegraphic Agency, as follows:

"To the great Jew and artist!

We thank you for your telegram of sympathy following the events of September 14 in our town. We want to tell you that your words of consolation strengthen our faith – and that of the entire Jewish nation – that the great wrongs done us will finally be recognized by humanity."

———

Translator's Footnotes:

1. The "Joint" (American Jewish Joint Distribution Committee) is a Jewish relief organization founded in 1914.
2. Translator's note: This was the most popular Polish–language Jewish newspaper in Poland, published daily between 1923 and September 1939.
3. I could not find any reference to a governor by this name; the governor of Bialystok between 1930 and 1937 was apparently named Stefan Kirtiklis.
4. The Yiddish daily *Undzer Lebn* was published in Bialystok in the 1930s.
5. I could not identify this name.
6. The daily newspaper *Haynt* was published in Warsaw from 1906 until 1939. The daily *Moment* was also published in Warsaw, from 1910 until 1939.

———

[Page 98]

The Trial

Translated by Yael Chaver

On February 17, 1937, the trial of the pogromists who rampaged against the Jews in Wysokie–Mazowieckie on September 14, 1936, began in the district court of Łomża. The judges were as follows: deputy president of the district court, Judge Sarkowski (Chief Justice), with judges Beblowski and Bandrzikowski. The prosecutor was Muszowski. Twenty hooligans were accused. The defenders were the infamous *Endecja* lawyers, B. Jerzowski and E. Mieczkowski. The civil prosecutors were the well–known Jewish lawyers, H. Erlikh of Warsaw, and Benyamin Groysbard of Łomża. The only defendant who did not appear was Jozefa Becker.

[Page 99]

Most of the defendants had no more than an elementary education, except for the main defendant, Jozef Wyszinski, who had completed four years of secondary school. There was another "intellectual" among the defendants: František Stawierew, an accountant at the farming cooperative in Dombrowka. Most of the defendants were peasants, except for one tailor, one construction worker, and Jadwiga Beker, a thief by profession. She was indeed brought to the court from prison.

The Bill of Indictment

"On September 14, 1936, during the fair held that day in Wysokie–Mazowieckie, members of the *Endecja* blocked the Christian population from shopping at Jewish–owned shops and stalls. The *Endeks* were organized in groups of three and five.

At first, their activity was relatively peaceful. However, in the afternoon, when thousands of peasants were at the fair, rioting began at the Jewish shops and stalls. On the one hand, some of the Christians were unwilling to follow the incitement of the *Endeks* and continued their shopping activity regardless of the tumult; on the other hand, the Jewish shopkeepers drove away the "boycott squads" from their shops.

At about four p.m., a loud whistle echoed through the market – a pre–arranged signal – and the fight crews attacked the Jewish–owned shops and stalls, shattering windows, and beating Jews.[1] The pogrom started simultaneously in various parts of the town.

It was difficult to control the situation under these conditions. When the police began to use rubber batons to disperse the rioting crowd, they were met with a hail of stones, shards of wood, and kitchen tools. Some police were injured. The rioting continued until 6:30 p.m.

...About 300 windows were broken and 1146 panes were shattered in 120 Jewish homes. Dozens of stalls were destroyed, and the wares in them were damaged. Thirty people were bruised, among them two gravely wounded.

The total damages to the Jewish population were estimated at about 6000 zloty."

* * *

The defendants, some of whom were well–known thugs and inciters, took an active part in overturning stalls, beating Jews, and flinging stones at the windows of Jewish homes and shops. There were three women were among the defendants: the above-mentioned Jozefa Beker, a thief; Zofia Leonjok; and Jadwiga Beker. They supplied the ruffians with stones, and helped to overturn stalls and break windowpanes.

[Page 100]

The prosecution brought over 70 witnesses, among them the governor of Wysokie, Dr. Jozef Świątkiewicz, as well as a number of high– and low–ranking police from Wysokie, and the police commissar of Wysokie county. The court has several medical certificates about Jews who were beaten and injured during the pogrom.

* * *

The account of the trial continues:

"After Judge Bandrzikowski read out the indictment, the defendants' statement were heard.

Defendant No. 1, Wyszinski, states that when he went into the *Endecja* office he did see several young people "politely" suggesting that the Christian customers not patronize Jews. Afterwards, when the crowd was rioting, he was not in the market, but in the house of an unknown woman named Szilewska. It is clear from his statements that he was the secretary of the *Endecja* in Dąbrówka.

Prosecutor Muszowski: If the defendant is innocent, as he states, why did he remain in hiding for four weeks?

Defendant Wyszinski: Because the police arrest "innocent people" every time there is an anti–Jewish operation. I did not want to be arrested, so I hid.

Attorney Erlikh (civil prosecution): Is the defendant only the secretary of the *Endecja* in Dąbrówka, or did he serve in the same capacity in Wysokie?

Wyszinski: I am also head of the Czyżew area.

Attorney Jerzerski (defense): Did Mr. Wyszinski receive an order from the party chairman, Attorney Jursz, to refrain from questionable exploits?

Wyszinski: Yes.

"The second defendant, Leon Dombrowski, stated that he is the county head of the *Endecja* in Wysokie–Mazowiecke, and that he received a letter from Party Chairman Jursz informing him that anti–Jewish "exploits" were being planned for September 14, and that he should not participate in them.

Attorney Graubard (defense): Did the defendant have a whistle?

Dombrowski: No.

"Defendants St. Tyminski and Jozef Kaczerowski state that, for two days, they had "noticed" youths preventing Christian customers from entering the Jewish–owned shops. Defendant Tomasz Zlotowski admits to lingering with the crowd, but only out of curiosity... Defendant Jozef Goloszewski admits inciting a boycott of the Jewish stores and preventing Christian customers from entering them, but that was all... He states that he saw overturned wagons that were full of merchandise, but that he does not know who the guilty party was. Defendant Stawierew states that he is a member of *Endecja*, and that he was in Wysokie–Mazowieckie on the day in question...but did not participate in the events.

[Page 101]

Attorney Graubard: Were you carrying a stick?

Stawierew: Yes.

Chief Justice Sarkowski: Was the operation organized?

Police Commissar Poprocki: Yes.

Chief Justice Sarkowski: Was it organized by the *Endecja*?

Police Commissar Poprocki: Yes, although the county head of the party published a declaration calling for calm.

Attorney Graubard: Did the declaration reach its addressees?

Commissar Poprocki: Yes.

Attorney Graubard: In that case, how did the pogrom happen after all?

Commissar Poprocki: The large numbers of young people had been incited.

Attorney Erlikh: Did Mr. Commissar hear that the pogrom was organized according to a system of "fives"?

Commissar Poprocki: Pickets.

Attorney Graubard: What is the difference between "pickets" and "fight crews"?

Commissar Poprocki: "Pickets" are quiet calls for a boycott. The "fight crews" use violence.

Attorney Graubard: Removing customers forcibly from a shop – would you call that "pickets" or "fight crews"?

Commissar Poprocki: There is no doubt that it was a "fight crew."

Attorney Graubard: Preventing customers from entering a shop – is that a "picket" or a "fight crew"?

Commissar Poprocki: (Embarrassed silence) "Pickets."

The other defendants responded similarly to the questions of the Jewish attorneys and the prosecutor.

* * *

After the statements of the defendants, the Court begins to hear the testimony of eyewitnesses. Most of them are common people, artisans, and owners of shops and stalls. In simple terms, they begin recounting the course of events. They identify most of the defendants as active participants in the pogroms, walking up to them, pointing at each, and saying their names.

The eyewitness statements of representatives of the Wysokie authorities and police were especially interesting.

The first witness was the deputy county governor, Jan Fronckewicz. He said that the county authorities had received credible information that a pogrom would break out in Wysokie on September 14, and added that the county governor, Dr. Świątkiewicz, had ordered the arrest of one man who had incited the youth to break windows. It became clear during the investigation that the man was Franciszek Stawierew, a name that he had often encountered in connection with *Endecja* activities. Among other things, Fronckewicz recounted that thanks to the intervention of the county governor, Dr. Świątkiewicz,

[Page 102]

the regional head of the *Endecja*, Attorney Jursz, sent a letter to party activists in Wysokie instructing them to refrain from acts of violence towards the Jewish population.

The next witness was Alexander Poprocki, formerly chief of police in Wysokie who was now the police commissar in Bialystok. He gave a detailed account of the course of events, describing how the county governor begged the crowd to refrain from "exploits." In answer to the *Endecja* attorneys, Poprocki notes that if the Jews had restrained themselves and not raised an outcry when a stall was overturned, the pogrom would not have reached such proportions.

Attorney Graubard responded immediately, asking him: "Mr. Commissar, do you think that if a person's stall is overturned – and furthermore, he receives a blow to the head – he does not have the right to cry out?" The embarrassed Poprocki replies, "Well, of course."

The lower–ranking police officers also give detailed accounts of the course of events that day, identifying and naming the defendants who participated in the pogroms.

* * *

After hearing the indictment, witness statements, and defense attorneys, the district court of Łomża ruled that five defendants should go free, for lack of evidence, and thirteen were sentenced to 6–10 months of imprisonment. All those convicted appealed the sentence.

The Trial in the Warsaw Appeals Court

The trial of the Wysokie pogromists in the Warsaw appeals court took place on September 1, 1937. The civil prosecutor representing the defendants was Erlikh. The *Endecja* hooligans, who were not present at the trial, were represented by attorney Jerszerski, a member of Nara.[2]

Prosecutor Jackiewicz proved that the defendants consistently used terror tactics and attacked innocent people, and that perpetrators of such crimes should be severely punished, and that the sentence passed in the district court of Łomża was too light for such acts of violence.

Attorney Erlikh's speech was brilliant. It included statements such as, "The fact that even though many stalls were overturned and their wares were damaged, and many shops were robbed, the damages did not exceed 6000 zloty, is clear evidence of the poverty of the Jewish population of Wysokie–Mazowieckie. This is the penniless population on which war was waged, in order to starve it. The pogromists' claim that the riots broke out because of Jewish provocation is both ridiculous and despicable. How can Jewish provocation be claimed, considering the fact that the Jews of Wysokie–Mazowieckie are only a small minority within a much larger Christian population?

"A boycott of Jews is not a new phenomenon in Poland. As early as in 1912, the notorious 'patriots' of Dmowski's school declared an economic boycott of the Jews of Poland. Then, too, Wysokie–Mazowieckie was a victim of that 'ultra–patriotic' operation." He went on to ask: "What is your right to declare an economic boycott of part of the population, of people who pay taxes and fulfil all their obligations to the authorities?!"

[Page 103]

Attorney Erlikh mocks the opinion of Poprocki, the police commander in Wysokie. Poprocki, who said in the district court of Łomża that if the Jews had not reacted by screaming, the riots would not have reached the dimensions they did. "How can one remain calm," says Erlikh sarcastically, "when shops are being looted, furniture is being broken, windowpanes are shattered, merchandise is damaged, and innocent people are beaten? Are people in this situation forbidden to raise their voices and scream?!"

He continues, referring to the statement of the Wysokie governor that boycott "pickets" are legal, and violence is the only thing that is prohibited. But we all know, adds the civil prosecutor, what the results of these "pickets" are. Furthermore, four weeks prior to the events, there were rumors in town that "something" would happen at the fair on September 14. It is therefore clear that the riots were pre–planned. In addition, according to the statements of the police witnesses the *Endeks* decided at their meeting to hold a "black wedding" in Wysokie–Mazowieckie on September 14.[3]

The defense's attorney, Nara member Jerszerski, reverted to the traditional *Endecdja* argument that the rioting in the town was caused by Jewish provocation. He did admit that pickets were standing near the Jewish shops, but that the leader of the *Endecja* youths warned picket members not to fall prey to the Jewish provocations. The *Endecja*, announced Jerszerski, boycotted the Jews not out of animosity but out of necessity. He quoted the classic statement of Premier Skladkowski, "Boycott –by all means!" Jerszerski claimed that the Jews were interested in causing an uproar in order to gain international support. The fair would have proceeded peacefully, were it not for the Jewish provocation.

The general prosecutor then spoke, refuting the ridiculous argument of "Jewish provocation." Breaking 300 windows is not an accident, and acts of violence must be punished.

After long deliberation, the appeals court ruled, confirming the verdict of the district court in Łomża concerning all the defendants, except for six. Because of their youthful age, their sentences would be carried out at a different time. The appeals court justified its verdict, arguing that the violent acts of the defendants were not necessary, contrary to the claims of the defense, and that the perpetrators of such acts must be punished. Therefore, all the defendants must serve their sentences.

(Information about both phases of the trial was taken from the Yiddish daily *Haynt* and the Hebrew weekly *BaDerekh*.)

———

Translator's Footnotes:

1. The writer uses the Slavic term *boyovka* for "fight crews."
2. The Nara organization was founded on April 14, 1934, by the militant youth wing of the *Endecja*. Its extremely anti-Semitic program was based on Hitlerism.
3. In Jewish tradition, a "black wedding" is performed at a time of crisis, such as an epidemic. The reference here is unclear but may imply a terrible disaster.

[Page 111]

Wysokie on the Eve of the Holocaust

Translated by Yael Chaver

September 1936. It was fair day in Wysokie. The market square was bustling with stalls and peasant wagons. The commotion was great.

Suddenly, pickets appeared at the Jewish shops. Young Polish men and women stood at the entrances and did not let the Polish peasants into the store.

These were the last days of my life in Poland, just before my emigration to the Land of Israel, after the major pogrom in Przytyk, and after the "By all means!" statement by the Polish premier, which permitted an economic boycott of Jews, and popularized the slogan "Poles buy only from Poles."[1] In theory, there was nothing new about the appearance of the boycott pickets at Jewish shops, but in actual fact, the Jews of Wysockie were shocked when this happened at their own shops.

I remember my mother's continued agitation: she knew several of the young women who picketed our shop: they came from well–off families, and were university students who had come town for their summer vacation. There was also a son of a family that did business with us; his father owned an estate, and had no commercial ties. My mother scolded them, telling to be ashamed of their deeds; but the young Poles were not ashamed. On the contrary, they viewed the boycott pickets as carrying out a Polish national mission. Someone yelled at our shop, "Go to Palestine!" At that moment I thought, "True, that is the solution that I chose. True, I had an immigration certificate (as a Hebrew University student), but the gates were closed to others. They faced a growing tide of anti–Semitism accompanied by an economic boycott."

Like the Jews in all other towns, the Jews of Wysokie found it difficult to accept the ever–increasing anti–Semitism, and tried to view it as a temporary aberration. However, the phenomenon was deeply rooted in Polish–Jewish reality. These roots had become evident in recent years, in changes that had occurred in the market: Polish-owned shops began to appear. Young men from peasant families were coming to the towns and trying their hand at commerce; when they discovered that Jews were more successful because they were more experienced, the "new shopkeepers" grew jealous of the Jews. Even more envious were "potential shopkeepers" who were planning to move from the villages.

Two years later, when I came to visit my parents, I found that the desire to undermine the success of others was expressed by a wave of mass demonstrations calling for war against Czechoslovakia. Feelings ran high, and people felt that the annexation of a small region would solve all of Poland's problems. All the young Poles of our town gathered at the Pilsudski monument in the market square, and swore to fight to the death for the liberation of Zaolzie.[2] Two years earlier, the monument had been the starting point for the pogrom against the Jews of Wysockie.

[Page 112]

The events of that Monday can hardly be called a pogrom, as the young Jews were not passive, and fought back against the hooligans. Actually, not too long before, when conscription was being conducted, Polish conscripts tried to riot and tear out the beard of a Jewish shop owner (I think it was Berish Tsukertszvayg, who owned a shoe store on the market street). Young Jewish men, including Fishke Yakovtshiner, Yeshayahu Perlman (the rabbi's son) and others, organized and showed the rioters that provoking the Jews was not worthwhile but could end in hospital; this was the case with several of the rioters. However, the rioters apparently did not learn their lesson. After they tried to attack the store of Zak and Zakimovitsh in order to drive away the Polish customers and rob it, and were chased off by Simkha Ze'ev Zak (who held them off with an iron bar), a whistle sounded. The pickets retreated, and immediately afterward attacked Ubagevitsh's stall, near the Pilsudski monument. Other Jewish stalls were also broken up, the merchandise scattered, and a hail of stones was directed at the Jewish houses. The great rampage began, while the police stood by helplessly. Many windowpanes were shattered, but the rioters were unable to enter the houses and rob them. Young Jews organized and drove the rioters away. Suddenly a shot rang out. The Poles claimed that the Jews had fired, but the Jews did not admit to that. In fact, however, the rioters scattered after the shot, taking their wounded with them.

A day or two later, a delegation of the JDC came to Wysokie, to examine the damages sustained by the Jews. The Jewish press published articles about the pogrom, which further depressed the spirits of the Jews in Wysokie. They felt that the Poles were undercutting their residence in the town, their livelihood, and their very existence. Even though the damages were not great, they felt that the world they had labored to create for generations had been destroyed.

The Jews of Wysokie could not accept this new reality, although signs of the approaching storm could be seen. For years, the Polish regime had not concealed its intentions to hamper the activities of Jewish shopkeepers and artisans, and thus destroy their livelihood. The pogroms were simply the extreme manifestation of the Jews' unstable situation. That was my feeling when I left Wysockie for the Land of Israel, the day after Rosh HaShana of 5697.[3] I first traveled to Constanta, Romania, and boarded the *Polonia* for the sea journey. There was another family from Wysockie on board: the Wiecha family, which was emigrating in its entirety, including the children, to join their family members in Hadera. I was **on my own**. Regardless of my joy at emigrating to the Land of Israel – which I had dreamed of and trained for – I was bothered by the thought that perhaps I was not doing the right thing by fleeing from a sinking ship. True, no one could have predicted the terrible catastrophe; but the thought that I was embarking on a new life while there, at home, I was leaving a family in a world that was bound for destruction, did not leave me throughout the sea trip.

At first glance, the country I was bound for, was also, of course, racked by riots.[4]

[Page 113]

The Arabs were on strike, attacking Jews, and there were skirmishes with Arab gangs. On the other hand, the home town that I had just left had suffered only some broken windows; but the feeling was different. My feeling proved justified. Although the riots in Palestine were still raging when I visited Wysokie in the fall of 1938, Europe was overshadowed by the Munich crisis, which was known in Poland as the Zaolzie crisis. Nationalist sentiment swelled in Poland.[5] Goering, Hitler's deputy, passed through Wysockie on his way to hunt in the Białowieża forests, and I was once again aware of the great tension among the town's Jews. They were consumed by the question of whether the Germans would be allies of Poland. Over the thoughts of an uncertain future loomed the present–day reality of impoverishment in families that were well off only a year or two earlier, and now faced want.

Friends who had stayed in the town sent very depressing reports of a decline in Jewish fortunes; this was in line with a seminar paper I had written the previous winter at the Hebrew University for Prof. Arthur Ruppin, about the increasing destitution of the Polish Jews.[6] As I gazed around me, I shuddered. At first, I thought that it was the contrast between the modern, spacious houses of Tel Aviv and Jerusalem and the wooden houses of Wysokie. However, it was the conversations with my friends in the youth movement: they all believed that there was no future. There was no hope for Wysokie, and the gates of Land of Israel were locked...

I began to view Wysokie differently than I had as a young person. This was a romantic, unhappy Wysockie. I sometimes think that the blue–painted wooden houses are sinking, and shrinking, and I hear the cry of young people seeking emigration to the Land of Israel for creativity and a better tomorrow.

———

Translator's Footnotes:

1. The Przytyk pogrom, perpetrated by Poles against Jews, occurred on March 9, 1936.
2. The area of Zaolzie is now in the Czech Republic
3. The date was September 26, 1936.
4. During 1936–1939 there were anti–Jewish and anti–British riots in Mandate Palestine. The period became known as "the Arab Revolt in Palestine."
5. On September 30, 1938, a settlement was reached in Munich, Germany, between Germany, Great Britain, France, and Italy that permitted German annexation of the Sudetenland, in western Czechoslovakia. It is widely regarded as an act of failed appeasement towards Germany, and a precursor of World War II.

6. Dr. Arthur Ruppin (1876–1943) was a Zionist thinker and leader, who founded the Department of Sociology at the Hebrew University

[Page 118]

Photographs

Translated by Yael Chaver

Card–players

Fair day in Wysokie

[Page 119]

Yo'irkeh, the water–carrier

[Page 120]

"Baron de Hirsch" the water carrier

[Page 121]

Khayim–Leib the Melamed and his kheyder

Alter the tailor

[Page 122]

Itzl, the wood–chopper

[Page 123]

Leybl Kiveyko, the fruit–seller

[Page 124]

"The Good–for–Nothing" play

"The Savage" play, directed by David Yakobi

[Page 125]

A cobbler and his apprentice

The children of the *Talmud Torah* having a meal, shortly after World War One

[Page 126]

Fragments of Memory

by Ya'akov Nitzevitsh–Nitzan

Translated by Yael Chaver

Bears and Monkeys

It was 1914, a few months before the war began, and I was still a small boy. I had just started to learn Torah with the *melamed* Efrayim, on Mistka Street. It was early spring, just before Purim. The snow was starting to melt, and the streets were full of mud and puddles trickling into the Brok River, which was filling fast and becoming a danger to people who lived nearby, especially on the Hintergas.[1]

The days were becoming warmer, and a new world was appearing before my child's eyes, a world full of wonders. I look forward impatiently to the green fields, to the reviving plants, to the forest of Zelig the miller, to birdsong, to the landowner's Turf River where I liked to bathe, and to the Szepietowo Road with its summertime crowds of men, women, and children.

On these spring days, I am confined (along with dozens of other children like me) to the small, stifling room that is the *kheyder* of Efrayim the *melamed*. I am forced to sit in front of the Torah. Occasionally, when my imagination escapes outdoors, to nature, freedom, and liberty – I feel the *rebbe*'s heavy slap on the back of my neck, and I must return to the gray, depressing reality of the *kheyder*.[2]

On one of those days, as I was deep in thought, as usual, a strange noise suddenly comes from outside; it grows stronger and stronger, until it becomes a deafening roar. Through the *kheyder* window, I see men, women, and children running to the marketplace, shouting the exciting news: "Bears and monkeys are in town!"

As you might imagine, no power in the world could stop us, the pupils of Efrayim the *melamed*, from leaving the *kheyder*. The *rebbe* locked the door, but in vain: some jumped through the window, others sneaked out through the back door. One way or another, the *kheyder* was instantly emptied, and all of Efrayim's students rushed to the marketplace.

In the market square, near the Fire Brigade's building (called "the shed"), the whole town was gathered. I doubt that anyone, except the babies and old people, stayed at home. I made my way through the crowd to the center of the marketplace, where the wonders were.

And it was indeed a marvelous sight. It was the first time I had ever seen these strange creatures. I have no words to describe the wonderful scene: the monkeys and the bears, skipping and dancing, eating out of human hands, and drinking from bottles. However, I was enthralled not only by the animals; their owners also captivated me. They seemed completely unlike the people in our town, in looks or clothing. Their legs were in high boots, laced from top to bottom; they wore green coats with red buttons, and their heads were covered by hats decorated with multicolored feathers.

[Page 127]

Unfortunately, I could not enjoy the scene for too long a time. I suddenly felt a sharp pain in my right ear. The pain grew stronger. When I turned my head to see the source of the pain, I saw the face of the *rebbe* Efrayim, whose delicate hand was pulling my ear. I don't need to tell you how much I hated the *rebbe* at that moment, especially when his calm, cruel voice said into my ear, in Yiddish, "Get going, *mamzer*, into the *kheyder*."[3] Escaping Efrayim was impossible. Ashamed, I was dragged back into the *kheyder*.

What can I tell you? I'm not a tattle-tale, so I will say only that I was in so much pain that night that I couldn't sleep, but tossed from side to side. When I finally fell asleep out of exhaustion, I was terrified by a nightmare. I wanted to scream, but could not. I was tongue-tied, until I finally gave out a terrible yell. My mother, who had heard the yell, leaped out of bed, lit the lamp and came over. I saw her frightened eyes as she looked at the black and blue bruises that *rebbe* Efrayim's fists had left all over my body; she began weeping bitterly.

It was not easy to convince my mother that it had only been a dream, a dream about bears and monkeys.

The Sleepless Night

Spring that year was over. At the height of summer, on the ninth day of Av – an ominous day – the war broke out.[4] The town was overtaken by gloom. People gathered everywhere–on the street, in the synagogue–speaking of one thing only: the war. Although the Jews hated *Fonye* bitterly and prayed for the defeat of the Russian forces, no one was joyful; all were heavy-hearted.[5]

The government announced a general conscription. There was weeping and wailing in the homes of conscripted husbands or sons. Before too long, the streets of Wysokie were filled with the first Russian troops, heading westward. An endless stream of infantry, cavalry, and horses pulling cannons, flowed through the town. Rumors soon began that the Germans were pushing the Russian army back and routing it. One major defeat occurred near Warsaw, and the Czarist forces began to retreat. The terrible news kept coming. Soon, the thundering of cannon could be heard in the town, indicating that the front was nearing Wysokie. One day, wagons loaded with wounded Russian soldiers, some with bandaged heads, came into the town. Heart rending moans came from the wagons. The Russian army was in full retreat.

[Page 128]

Like other towns along the Bialystok–Warsaw route, Wysokie provided temporary lodgings for the retreating Russian army; the town was full of military personnel. Soldiers and officers were billeted in most homes. Our house, with its four rooms, housed stunned officers who were awaiting new retreat orders from the High Command. One evening, as we were sitting with them, tense and anxious about the future, a trumpet call sounded outside. By now, we knew that trumpet calls did not bode well for the Russian army. And indeed, the officers left their seats and hurried outside at the command of a senior officer. The last officer to leave instructed us to turn off the lights immediately and lie flat on the floor. He parted from us on friendly terms and thanked us for our generosity towards the "guests." The door closed behind him as he left.

The house grew very silent. We turned off the lights and lay on the floor, trembling in fear. Outside, we could hear the rumble of wheels and the sound of the hooves of the horses that were pulling the heavy cannons of the retreating Russian army. The whistling of bullets and shells was heard from time to time; their flashes penetrated the closed shutters. We followed the events outside with bated breath. The noise and explosions increased, and the thundering of the cannons and other weapons grew deafening. We crept closer together and became a single living entity of flesh and blood, of frightened children and a devoted mother who was protecting her children with her body, like an eagle protecting its young.

We lay on the floor for many hours. Much later that night, certainly after midnight, we felt that the terrifying orchestra was becoming weaker. The cannon thunder grew more and more distant, and finally fell silent. Wysokie was enveloped in a stunning, deathly silence. The first light of day began to be seen through the chinks in the shutters. A new day was born.

We slowly went to the door and opened it a crack. The German advance forces appeared on Mistka Street. The first German rider sat his horse with complete calm, crossing the street carefully back and forth, like a night watchman not wanting to disturb the sleepers. He was followed by cavalry, and later the infantry.

The townspeople emerged from their hideouts to see these saviors who would liberate them from the tyrannical Czar; after all, during World War I the Germans were considered to be liberators from the despotic Czarist regime. With combined joy and fear, the Jews received the German army and gave them all the cakes and *challahs* that were ready for Shabbat (the Germans had entered the town on a Friday morning). However, they were very disappointed when the soldier and officer "saviors" rejected the Jewish presents and greeted the donors with the curse *verfluchte Jude* (damned Jew).

The cool, hostile attitude of the Germans cooled the Jews' enthusiasm; they soon discovered that these were not saviors. It is worth noting, however, that during World War I the German soldiers did not commit robbery and murder. Their attitude

[Page 129]

of these solders was restrained and proper. The authorities immediately started to establish a new order according to the German system. They started building a modern hospital, planted trees along the streets, opened a large bath–house; and the town began to change.

The new conditions, with its few positive, and many negative notes, lasted until the end of the war. When the enormous war machine of the German Reich was destroyed, the Germans left the soil of Poland, and were replaced by the Poles, who immediately instituted a policy of hostility towards the Jewish population.

————

Translator's Footnotes:

1. The Yiddish "Hintergas" means "Back Street."
2. *Rebbe* is the term for a *kheyder* teacher; it is also used for a Hasidic leader.
3. The Hebraic *mamzer* ("bastard") is used as a derogatory term for a difficult or unpleasant individual.
4. World War I broke out on August 1, 1914. It was also the ninth day of the Jewish month of Av, a fast day commemorating numerous historic national cataatrophes.
5. Original note: *Fonye* is a derogatory Jewish term for the Russian Czar.

————

[Page 129]

Two Poems

by Sarah Tuvia

Translated by Yael Chaver

On the Death of My Father

My father, you are no more. My father is dead.
I am glad I told you, "My good father."
You were good, my father. So good.
That is why my dreams were bright
And my waking full of music.
You taught me ethics through the sayings of Hillel,
Through legends of Elisha Ben Avuya,
Of Rabbi Elazar ben Arakh,
Through the sayings of Rabbi Akiva
And your sorrowful look.[1]
My father is no more.
He walked slowly,
Cloaked in the majesty of his tall father,
His eyes spread understanding
And his brows express compassion.
Now he is gone. Dead.
The images of childhood mourn,
Mourn.
The vision of legends is orphaned
From father's knee.

Nissan 1932[2]

[Page 130]

To My Mother

The mean whiles are so long My mother!
I send you this card
With only a few words:
"I don't know which world I am addressing."
It is very hard to write, Mother!
Will the post bring letters again
As before, saying that you are well
And that nothing has changed at home?
That you are very happy to receive
My frequent letters.
Let my words be calm and wise,
But only one short phrase between the lines–
About my father, who died. I am very sad without him.

My heart is very anxious, Mother!
1941

———

Translator's Footnotes:

1. The names are of post–biblical Jewish sages.
2. The Jewish month of Nissan typically occurs in late March – early April.

[Pages 130-137]

Jablonka Koscielna

[120.7 kilometers NE of Warsaw]

52° 57' / 22° 22'

Jablonka My Shtetl

by Arie Wajsbord

Translated by Ada Holtzman z"l

In the middle of the road between Wysokie to Zambrow, on the right side, in the middle of a small valley - Jablonka, my little town exists. Three streets were in Jablonka, and 90% of it were Jews. The street which leads to Wysokie Mazowiecki was called "Podlasia"; the street to zambrowa was named "Moza" and the half a circle between the two streets was named the "Rynek" (the Market square).

From a distance the three streets resembles an eagle, and since nearby was the river "Raczka Jablon" (and from this derived the name of town Jablonka), the shtetl had the image of an eagle landing from the heights to drink fresh and pure waters.

According to the sources Jews came to Jablonka long time before their settlement in the beighbouring towns. Testimony of this fact is the old cemetry with the large trees which no more thicken and frozen they stand with their enourmous heads, like guards keeping the remains of Kosher Jews who buried in the *Kever Israel* (grave of Israel) for many generatins. In the Yizkor book of Lomza, Yom Tov Lewinski writes that when Zambrow, the town near Jablonka, was founded, the deceased of zambrow were buried in Jablonka, until the town grew bigger and with many efforts, the community of Zambrow got the permission to sanctify its own Jewish cemetery. In addition, it was the custom to arrange divorce ceremony in Jablonka, because it had the river running all the year, while in Wysokie it got dried in the summer time.

The estate of the Kulesze was on a few dunams, and considred as a holy site. This is because of a legend which passed from generation to generation in Jablonka, that in this place, on the old foundations of the old synagogue which was destroyed during

WWI, a new holy site will be erected. And we, the children, dreamt and hoped to see the new synagogue with blue windows stand again, and pigeons, as the old people said, will sing their beautiful tunes once again.

The Jews of Jablonka were modest and hard laborers, who worked hard for their livelihood and were connected to the land from which they made their living. They fulfilled all their duties as citizens of Poland, and were totally devoted to the Zionist idea. We did not have revolutionaries and nor Epicureans. During a dry year the Jews of Jablonka prayed for rain and in over flooded year they prayed for bright blue skies.

Although it was a very small, our shtetl was blessed with intellectuals such as Bril and Szmule Slotka and Mendel Kroliwecki of blessed memory, the "doctor" who cured for free also Gentile people.

In Jablonka there were pioneer youth who went to *Hachshara* places (places of preparatory for immigration to *Eretz Israel*) and during years they prepared for immigration so that they weill be useful and constructive citizens in the Land of Israel. And there were young men in Jablonka, who, as there were no *Yeshiva* (*Talmudic* college) in town, wandered to far away *Yeshivas* all over Poland and Lithuania to study the *Torah*. When they returned to the shtetl, with the Zionist ideals penetrated into them, they spread the idea of the national revival in Eretz Israel among the youth and the adult people. They participated in public shows, participated in public ardent debates about subjects of paramount concern and sung the songs of Zion. Often the passionate arguments reached high tones, especially when orators from *Poalei Zion* and other parties came from Zambrow and Wysokie. Even though these verbal fights seemed so deep, it never was accompanied by any hostility to the opponent. As these debates were for heaven sake, and afterwards the opponents remained friend as before. Because everybody knew that even if the roads are different' they all lead to the same goal. Until today I remember the spiritual pleasure which we derived from sitting with our *"Yeshiva"* young men.

Jablonka was a distinguished Zionist shtetl. In every home you could find the blue box of Keren Kayemet Le'Israel (The Jewish National Fund), and during every event, funds were collected for *Eretz Israel*. Every cultural event with any income, part of it was allocated to the *Keren Kayemet*, and every bet or a vow, the money was donated to it or the *Keren Hayesod* – the Foundation Fund.

The economic life of the Jews of Jablonka resembled more the life style of a *Moshav Ovdim* (communal settlement in Eretz Israel) than the Jewish shtetl in Poland. Each Jew had a vegetable garden and also fruit trees. Nearly every family had a cow and everyday there was someone else who took the herd to the pasture and return it in the evening. The fee of the shepherd was paid collectively. When the time to collect potatoes arrived (since every Jew took care of having a cellar full of potatoes for the whole year, whether it was his own filed or leased one), the work was done collectively in turn. Everyday people were gathered at someone's field who prepared *"Tluka"* and together they filled tens of sacks with the collected potatoes.

Similar happening was in pulling feathers during the night following the *Sabbath*. This became a source of joy. In Jablonka nearly every family had an auxiliary farm, especially poultry: hens, ducks and goose. The goose and ducks were fattened and while they were fat enough, the *Shochet*, (ritual slaughterer) who was my uncle from Wysokie, was called to butcher them. The fat was melted during the long winter nights and the feathers were pulled and cushions and pillows their were filled with them. These pillows were given to young maidens as part of their dowry. Also filling the cushions was done together in good company. The housewife fried *"latke"*, pancakes with sugar and fritters were eaten without an end, each one as much as he liked. Often such a *"tluka"* ended by dawn.

These frequent gatherings inspired the shtetl with good atmosphere of family warmth. Everyone cared for his fellowship and was interested with his friend's well being and the whole shtetl seemed to be one big family.

Without artists and entertainers, our townspeople knew to rejoice and fill their lives with folkloristic hearty meaning. Take for example the *Sabbath* (Saturday) when they whole shtetl received a groom who came to visit his bride from another place. As soon as the prayer of *Mussaf* had ended, the children rushed, red were their faces from excitement, to bring the *Cholent*. By the end of the meal, they were sent with a bottle of liqueur to the house of the future father-in-law (only children were allowed to carry anything during the holy *Sabbath*). And in the house of the future father-in-law, tables were prepared with drinks and refreshments: fruits, hazelnuts and sweets from Eretz Israel...

During the evening, all those who sent drinks to the house of the future father-in-law gathered and around led tables greeting and wishes were said to the engaged couple and their parents. People ate, drunk, sung and recited poems and prayers and everybody participated in their fellowman's happiness. These fests contributed a lot to the success of the matchmaking than the dowry.

Also secular days were full of joy and festivities. While our dramatic circle showed a play, many visitors from Zambrow and Wysokie, Wizna and Kulesze Koscielne and all the neighboring small villages where Jews lived came to see it and enjoyed the opportunity of meeting of other Jews from other shtetls.

Gone is Jewish Jablonka. Our little shtetl was erased off the earth like hundreds of other communities in Europe. After the War I had sent a letter of inquiry to Mr. Zaloski, my Polish teacher. He wrote to me that the Jews of Jablonka stayed for a short time in ghetto Wysokie, and together with the Jews of Zambrow they were deported and perished in Auschwitz. From the Polish population, the teacher Jazombek and the policeman Bagonski were killed.

After the receipt of this letter, my last hope ended. There are no more Jews in Jablonka. Father perished, Mother perished, brothers and sister perished. The cruel enemy murdered them all – people, women, children. And a frightful cry emersed from the depth of the heart: *W H Y?!*

The Jewish youth in Jablonka

The library Committee in Jablonka

[Page 138]

Notable Rabbis and Scholars in Wysokie–Mazowieckie

by Moshe Tsinovitsh

Translated by Yael Chaver

Rabbi *Gaon* Meir HaLevi Hurvits[1]

There are few sources about the life and work of Rabbi *gaon* Meir HaLevi Hurvits. He appears for the first time as the rabbi and head of the rabbinical court in Wysokie–Mazowieckie in 1833, in connection with the publication of *Avot DeRabi Natan* together with the commentaries *Sheney Avraham* and *Ben Avraham*, by Rabbi Eliyahu (son of Avraham) of Delyatitsh (Nowy Grod district). Rabbi Meir HaLevi Hurvits of Wysokie was one of the renowned rabbis and rabbinical scholars who approbated its publication.

Rabbi Meir HaLevi died in 1852 or 1853. He is mentioned in a eulogy by Rabbi *gaon* Yosef Khaver, head of the rabbinical court of Knyszyn and Jedwabne, who was eulogizing his father Rabbi *gaon* Yitzchak–Ayzik Khaver, head of the rabbinical court of Tykocin and Suwalki. Rabbi Yosef Khaver was also eulogizing Rabbi Meir HaLevi Hurvits and the rabbis and *gaons*Aryeh–Leyb Shapira, head of the rabbinical court of Kaunas, and Eliezer Yitzchak Frid, head of the rabbinical court and rabbi in Volozhin, both of whom had also died that year.

Rabbi Khanokh Zundt of Bialystok, author of *HaAnafim*, also writes of Rabbi Meir HaLevi: "The honored rabbi, as bright as the sun, famous, righteous, and modest...labors day and night studying the holy Torah, hates greed, and is busy with charity and aid..."

These eulogies by rabbis and *gaons* are evidence that Rabbi Meir HaLevi Hurvits, besides being a great scholar, was modest and unassuming, righteous, charitable, cared for the poor, and was a faithful shepherd of his flock.

Rabbi *Gaon* Eliezer Shlomo Veler

The long work *Berit Olam* by his son, Rabbi Ayzik Ya'akov Veler, contains the following details about his life and work:

Rabbi Eliezer Shlomo came from a large family of *gaons* and righteous men. He was a grandson and great–grandson of the famous *gaons* Rabbi Reuven, head of the rabbinical court in Bialystok, and of the *gaon* and righteous man Yosef, author of Rosh Yosef (a commentary on several tractates) who was the son–in–law of the famous *gaon* Rabbi Moshe Kremer, head of the rabbinical court in Vilna. The author of *Berit Olam* adds, "I heard from my beloved father and teacher, the *gaon* (may his righteous memory be for a blessing) that his ancestors could trace their lineage to the holy Rashi."[2]

It should be added that for a time Rabbi Yosef was the chief religious judge in the community of Tykocin, near Wysokie. His father–in–law, Rabbi Moshe Kremer, came from the family of the Vilna *gaon* (Rabbi Eliyahu of Vilna).[3]

[Page 139]

Rabbi Eliezer Shlomo Veler was head of the Wysokie rabbinical court for forty years (1852–1892), and was renowned in this community and its surroundings.

Rabbi *Gaon* Ayzik Ya'akov Veler

Rabbi Ayzik Ya'akov was born in Wysokie in 1856, to his father, Rabbi *gaon* Eliezer Shlomo and his mother Miriam, the daughter of the *gaon* Rabbi Yitzkhak–Ayzik Khaver, head of the rabbinical courts in Ruzhany, Vawkavysk, Tykocin, and Suwalki, where he died in 1853. Rabbi Ayzik Ya'akov was named after his maternal grandfather. His teacher of Torah and commandments was his father, the local rabbi, as he himself recounted in his book *Berit Olam*.

When he was of marriageable age, he married the daughter of Ya'akov (son of Shim'on) Mushkin of Kletsk (Slutsk district, Minsk province). He stayed in Kletsk after the wedding, and studied Torah in the large House of Study there. That was also where he gained expertise in Jewish law, from the local Rabbi *gaon* Shalom Dov Hernzon.

Sometimes, when he came to see his father, he would spend some time with his uncle, the Rabbi *gaon* Moshe Rabinovitsh, head of the rabbinical court of Jedwabne. When he stayed with his uncle, he served as a legal authority, and also helped him organize the writings of his father, the *gaon* Rabbi Yitzchak Ayzik and his uncle, the *gaon* Rabbi Yosef Khaver, who preceded him as the head of the rabbinical court of Jedwabne.

When his father, Rabbi Eliezer Shlomo, died in 1892, Rabbi Ayzik Ya'akov was appointed the town rabbi of Wysokie. At first, the hasidim opposed him, as the Veler family – like that of the *gaon* Rabbi Yitzkhak–Ayzik Khaver and both of his sons – Yosef and Moshe – were extreme *misnagdim*.[4] However, before too long, the hasidim, too, came to like and admire the young rabbi. In addition to his intellectual ability and knowledge of the Torah, he had outstanding qualities and a pleasant temperament; these moderated the resistance to his position.

In 1896, his book *Berit Olam* appeared; it comprised responsa to the four sections of the *Shulkhan Arukh*. This work made him renowned among the great rabbis and heads of *yeshiva*s at the time. His commentaries and explanations are very clear, and help to clarify the most difficult issues. He gained the approbation and admiration of the great rabbis of the area, including the *gaons* Rabbi Malkiel Tenenbaum, head of the rabbinical court of Łomża (author of the *Divrey Malkiel* responsa), and Rabbi Eliyahu Barukh Kamey, head of the rabbinical court of Ciechanowice and later head of the renowned Mir *yeshiva*.

According to *Berit Olam*, he corresponded with the greatest scholars of Jewish law, as well as with commentators on Talmudic issues. Among the best known of these were the *gaon* Rabbi Khayim HaLevi Soloveichik, head of the Volozhin *yeshiva* and later head of the rabbinical court of Brest–Litovsk in Lithuania, and later with his relative, Rabbi Mordekhai Białobłocki, of Valfi (Grodno Region).[5]

[Page 140]

Rabbi Ayzik Ya'akov Veler died after a major illness in the same year that his book was published; he was only forty years old.

Three rabbis eulogized him: Rabbi Shimon Dov Anulik, head of the rabbinical court of Tykocin; Rabbi Dov Menakhem Regensberg, head of the rabbinical court of Dąbrowa, and Rabbi Menakhem Yonah Gitelman, head of the rabbinical court of Sokoły. All the shops in Wysokie were closed on the day of his funeral, and the artisans stopped work.

Rabbi Aharon Ya'akov Perlman (may God avenge his blood)

The last rabbi of Wysokie–Mazowieckie was born in the town of Horodok, in Vilna County. He was one of the outstanding students of the renowned Volozhin *yeshiva*; as a youth, he studied with the two great heads of this illustrious *yeshiva*: the *gaon* Rabbi Naftali Zevi Yehuda Berlin (known by the acronym Natziv), and the *gaon* Rabbi Khayim Soloveichik.[6]

In addition to being an outstanding scholar, Rabbi Perlman was also famous for his wisdom, his ethical character, and his good manners. He married a daughter of the distinguished Bunimovich family of Volozhin, famous throughout Lithuania. After his marriage, he studied for several years in a special *kollel* within the Volozhin *yeshiva* that was earmarked for outstanding scholars who came recommended.[7] The *kollel* was funded by Yisra'el Brodsky, the renowned Jewish millionaire of Kiev, who willed a specific sum for the purpose, under the management of his son Lazar. When the millionaire Lazar Brodsky once met the young Rabbi Aharon Ya'akov Perlman, he was very impressed, and gladly continued to support the *kollel* in Volozhin.

After the death of Rabbi Ayzik Ya'akov Veler, there was heated debate among the leaders of the Jewish community of Wysokie about the selection of a new rabbi.

The *misnagdim* defeated the hasidim; they insisted on selecting a rabbi who would follow the Lithuanian tradition. The *gaons* Rabbi Hirshl Rabinovitch (head of the rabbinical court of Kaunas) and Rabbi Moshe Danishevski (head of the rabbinical court of Slobodka), decided, with the approval of the aged Rabbi Shmuel Mohilever (head of the rabbinical court of Bialystok), to select Rabbi Aharon Ya'akov Perlman as rabbi and head of the rabbinical court of Wysokie–Mazowieckie.

Rabbi Perlman was an excellent choice. During the forty years that he served as rabbi in Wysokie, he fulfilled his role as the spiritual leader of the community and the town rabbi, with great success and devotion. He became famous throughout the region, and was consulted by rabbis of the surrounding towns about secular matters as well as religious issues. Rabbi Perlman was a gifted Hebrew writer, and had good knowledge of Russian, the language of the authorities. He was active in the community, a fine preacher, and was well–loved by the community. He also became renowned as an expert in religious law and a mediator in disputes. Various communities – mainly from the Łomża and Bialystok areas – asked him to arbitrate, and his decisions were fully accepted by all parties. The following incident in Jedwabne is an example.

[Page 141]

Rabbi Aharon Ya'akov Perlman
(may God avenge his blood)

In 1926, a severe dispute broke out between one faction of the community and the local ritual slaughterer. The head of the rabbinical court, Rabbi Avigdor Bialostotsky, was unable to make peace between the sides, and it was decided to ask Rabbi Perlman to judge. The Rabbi of Wysokie spent a full week in Jedwabne. After he had listened to both sides and heard various witnesses, he returned to Wysokie and sent his opinion (with the agreement of Rabbi Avigdor Bialostotsky) with special instructions for the ritual slaughterer concerning his continuing work in the town. Characteristically, both parties accepted his verdict, and followed all its sections, according to Rabbi Perlman's instructions.

Rabbi Perlman was a Lover of Zion from his time as a student in the Volozhin *yeshiva*, and was always very interested in the Zionist movement and the new Jewish community in the Land of Israel.[8] He was a member of the Zionist movement, and voted for the *Mizrachi* party. However, for tactical reasons, he never joined that party officially, did not participate in Zionist conventions, and was not active in Zionist affairs. His reasoning was that, as the rabbi of the community, he had to be devoted to the entire community, regardless of its factions, and not exhibit sympathy towards any particular political party. On the other hand, he was very active in public areas that were directly connected with religious life and his rabbinical responsibilities. In 1910, he participated in the convention of the rabbis of Łom&#ża County, which had to elect a delegate to the national convention of rabbis in St. Petersburg; the delegate was Rabbi Malkiel Tenenboym, head of the rabbinical court of Łom&#ża. He also took part in the rabbinical convention of 1916, during the German occupation of World War One. He presided over both conventions, and had great influence over all the topics discussed at these conventions.

[Page 142]

When Polish sovereignty was restored, he was active in Bialystok County. He participated in many conventions aimed at strengthening Judaism in independent Poland, and was one of the leaders who fought for protecting the rights of Jews, when these rights were being diminished by the central and regional authorities. When the economic boycott of Polish Jews strengthened in the late 1930s, and pogroms broke out against Jews in Wysokie–Mazowieckie (1936), Rabbi Perlman was one of the chief leaders who did their best to curb the damages inflicted on the Jewish community by the crowds and the authorities. He was active in various institutions in Bialystok and in Warsaw aiding those affected by the pogroms, and was in close contact with the JDC.

Rabbi Aharon Ya'akov Perlman continued to be a faithful leader and shepherd during the disasters that overtook the Jews of Europe during World War Two. He stayed with his flock until the very last moments of the catastrophe. He was in the Wysokie ghetto and the Zambrów camp, and surrendered Wysokie his pure, holy soul in Auschwitz, along with the thousands of Wysokie Jews who died in the gas chambers of the Nazis, may their names be blotted out. May God avenge his blood.

Rabbi and Auxiliary Rabbi Yisr'ael Khayim Olsha[9]

Rabbi Yisra'el was born in Sokoły, near Wysokie. His father was one of the community's leaders and a hasidic leader as well. He studied at the Łom&#ża yeshiva, and at the Kaunas kollel. He married the daughter of the Rabbi of Sokoły, the gaon Rabbi Mordechai (Sender's son).

He was a great expert in biblical law and issues of permission and prohibition, as well as in official government law; he was familiar with worldly and commercial matters. His appointment as auxiliary rabbi in Wysokie–Mazowieckie was seen as compensation to the local hasids, whose numbers and public influence was constantly increasing.

Rabbi Yisra'el Khayim Olsha's life was short. His death at an early age was a blow to the town's Jews. The greatest rabbis of the region participated in his funeral and gave eulogies.

[Page 143]

Rabbi Gershon Broide (may his memory be for a blessing)

He came to Lithuania as a young man, and soon became renowned for his scholarship as well as for his influence over the young scholars who clustered around the gaon Rabbi Ayzik Ya'akov Veler, author of Berit Olam. He soon became famous throughout the region as a brilliant young intellectual; rabbis and heads of yeshivas discussed Jewish law with him. He married the daughter of Rabbi Simkha HaKohen Kaplan, one of the important householders of the town, who liked his daughters to marry famous scholars.

Rabbi Gershon Broide was a long–time Lover of Zion, and had even known one of the founders of that movement, Rabbi Shmuel Mohilever (head of the rabbinical court of Bialystok), with whom he had had long conversations about religious matters and settlement in the Land of Israel. When Theodor Herzl founded the Zionist organization, Rabbi Broide was one of the organizers of a local Zionist group in Wysokie. Most members of this group were scholars.

When the Mizrachi opened a branch in Wysokie (1918), he joined that national–religious movement and was one of its ideological leaders. The fact that Rabbi Broide joined the Mizrach influenced the ultra–religious community as well as many of Wysokie's hasidic Jews, who were concentrated in the synagogues of the Ger and Aleksander hasidic groups.[10]

In 1917, in parallel with the Balfour Declaration, the Zionist Central Committee in Warsaw sent a petition to the authorities of Germany and Austria – the two powers of the Central Alliance – to recognize the rights of the Jews to the Land of Israel.[11] He left Wysokie after the death of his wife, married the widow of Rabbi Magentsa, and was appointed Rabbi of Suwalki.

Rabbi Broide died suddenly in one of the houses of study in Lithuania, while it was full of people. This was during World War Two, when the Germans started exterminating the Jews in *Aktions*; he was delivering a eulogy for the Jewish community of Suwalki, when he suddenly collapsed and died.[12]

Rabbi Ya'akov Slodki (may God avenge his memory)

One of the most important religious figures of Wysokie–Mazowieckie was Rabbi Ya'akov Slodki (better known as Ya'akov, Levi's son). He was an auxiliary rabbi, and often participated in religious court processes. He substituted for the local rabbi in case of need.

He was a great scholar, and would study two pages of Talmud daily at the Ger synagogue. His study partner was the learned Rabbi Alter Gorzelczany. He was very astute, had a fine voice, and served as cantor during the High Holidays.

[Page 144]

Rabbi Eliezer (Leyzer) Yehuda Boiman

(may God avenge his blood)

He set an example for the entire town: he was unusually observant, scholarly, modest, and honest. People who wanted to emphasize the character of a person who was decent and observant would use Rabbi Leyzer Yehuda as an example. In spite of his poverty, he always radiated joy, and inspired those who were depressed and needed encouragement.

The writer Menakhem Mendel Litevka

Menakhem Mendel Litevka was born in Wysokie–Mazowieckie in 1856. Like most other Jewish boys of the time, he was educated in traditional *kheyders* in his town. As there was no *yeshiva*in Wysokie, he went on to Bialystok and studied the Talmud and commentaries (Rashi and later commentators) in that city's *yeshiva*.

It was there that he became acquainted with Asher (son of Khava), who introduced him to the world of enlightenment and Hebrew teaching. He started as a private tutor in Hebrew and Bible for the rich Frumkin family, who owned an estate near Wysokie-Mazowieckie.

He came to Warsaw in 1891, bearing a recommendation from the Frumkins to wealthy Lithuanian Jews who had moved to Warsaw. These Jews, though adhering to Jewish commandments and tradition, were aware of the new trends among Jews, especially in the large cities, and wanted to teach their children the basics of Hebrew and Hebrew literature, in addition to religious studies. Several of these families hired Litevka as a tutor.

In Warsaw, he began to publish poems and epigrams in Hebrew–language publications, especially in *HaTsfira*, where he published a series of *feuilletons* with the general title "From Here and There."

His book *HaZamir* –a collection of poems and epigrams – appeared in 1895, thanks to the assistance of his friend M. B. Rozen, another native of Wysokie. Rozen was a successful businessman in Warsaw who was friendly with Hebrew writers, and supported young Jews who had left the world of religious studies and come to Warsaw for a general secular education. Rozen himself had a broad education and was a writer in his own right; he wrote the introduction to Litevka's book, in which he praised the talent of the latter as a writer and intellectual.

HaZamir consisted of 48 poems and 60 epigrams, which were unusually witty and pointed. Although most of Litevka's work was just versification rather than true poetry, he used clear language, and young people enjoyed them. Especially remarkable were the poem "Moses Did not Die" (commemorating Baron de Hirsch), a poem dedicated to the famous German writer Lessing (a friend of Moses Mendelssohn's), and poem about his love for Jerusalem.

[Page 145]

Litevka became ill during World War One, and could no longer support himself by teaching. Some of his former students helped him a bit financially, and he was able to live, though very modestly. The support was organized by the famous rabbi and scholar Dr. Shmuel Avraham Poznanski.

Menakhem Mendel Litevka died in 1920, at age 65. *HaTsfira* published the following brief eulogy (no. 16, 1920): "Mr. Menakhem Mendel Litevka has died at age 65. He was a teacher, a Hebrew writer and poet, and one of the last old–style scholars."

His book *HaZamir* is in the Jewish National Library of Jerusalem, with the following handwritten dedication by the author: "Fondly dedicated to the renowned scholar of rich and varied achievement, Dr. Sh. Poznanski, by his admirer, the author."

———

Translator's Footnotes:

1. The Hebrew term *gaon* (brilliant scholar, genius) is often appended to the name of a well–regarded rabbi.
2. Shlomo Yitzchaki (1040 – 1105), today generally known by the acronym *Rashi* (see below), was a medieval French rabbi and author of a comprehensive commentary on the Talmud and commentary on the Hebrew Bible. His work is used to this day.

3. Elijah ben Solomon Zalman (1720–1797), known as the Vilna *Gaon* or Elijah of Vilna, was a Talmudist, halakhist, kabbalist, and the foremost leader of non–hasidic Jewry of the past few centuries

4. The *misnagdim* (literally, "opponents") were members of a movement that resisted the rise of Hasidism. They were particularly concentrated in Lithuania, with Vilna as their center.

5. Brest–Litovsk is now in Belarus. I was not able to identify the town of Valfi.

6. The Volozhin *yeshiva* was a prestigious Lithuanian *yeshiva* located in Volozhin (now Valozhyn, Belarus). It was founded by a student of the Vilna Gaon, and trained generations of scholars, rabbis, and leaders. Completed in 1806, it was the first modern *yeshiva* and served as a model for all *yeshiva*s that later opened in Lithuania.

7. The *kollel* is an advanced group for full–time, advanced study of the Talmud and rabbinic literature.

8. The "Lovers of Zion" (*Hovevei Tziyon*) was a group of organizations that were founded in 1881 in response to the Anti–Jewish pogroms in the Russian Empire, and were officially constituted as a group in 1884, with the aim of promoting Jewish immigration to Palestine and advancing Jewish settlement there. They are considered the forerunners and foundation–builders of modern Zionism.

9. A rabbi specializing in Jewish religious law (*moreh–tzedek*) in a community is sometimes termed an "auxiliary rabbi."

10. The Ger hasidic group was founded by Yitzkhak Meir Alter (1798–1866) in the town of Góra Kalwaria, Poland. It is one of the largest and most influential hasidic groups today. The Aleksander hasidic group originated from the city of Aleksandrow Lodzki, Poland, in the early 19th century, and was second only to the Ger group in numbers before World War Two.

11. The Balfour Declaration was a a public statement issued by the British government in 1917 announcing support for the establishment of a "national home for the Jewish people" in Palestine, then an Ottoman region.

12. *Aktions* were German mass operations to round up Jews before deporting and murdering them.

[Page 145]

Jewish Personalities

Translated by Yael Chaver

Khayim Bar–Nakhum (may his memory be for a blessing)

He was known in Ben–Shemen as "Khayim–from–heaven," for his amazingly modest and frugal life and his altruism and utter devotion to his students.[1] His great gifts as an educator, who developed an original educational method and saved dozens of neglected and oppressed children from a life of ethical decline; the radiance that shone from his warm personality towards all his friends and acquaintances – all these made Khayim Bar–Nakhum a noble, pure–hearted person, who was much admired.

[Page 146]

Berl Katznelson, who recognized his worth, said: "I knew two wondrous personalities, who resembled each other, during my life in the Land of Israel: Y. Kh. Brenner, and Khayim Bar–Nakhum."[2]

He was born about 74 years ago in Jedwabne, near Łomża. During World War One, he lived and taught in Wysokie. When the war ended, he moved to Lithuania and joined the educators of the Kaunas Orphanage, headed by leadership of Dr. Lehmann.[3] The desperate children, all war refugees, quickly became attached to their teacher, and were ready to follow him anywhere. When it came time for all the Orphanage residents –students and teachers – to emigrate to the Land of Israel, Khayim went ahead, to scout out a proper site. He welcomed the first group of students; at first, they settled on the property of Moshe Smilansky, where they worked by day and studied by night.[4] When Ben–Shemen was established, they moved to their permanent location.

Khayim worked as a teacher and educator in Ben–Shemen for many years. He strove to have the institution function as a kibbutz of educators and youth. When his idea was rejected, he left Ben–Shemen, gathered abandoned children from all over the country, and returned to the vicinity of Ben–Shemen with them. They lived in tents, as a "family kibbutz," in which educators and children worked and studied together, while acquiring modest and ethical life habits.

The experiment succeeded: his great pedagogic gifts and personal example of simplicity and ethics influenced these children, who found their way to lead productive lives.

Khayim never created a family of his own, but his students form a family that lives throughout Israel, constantly remembering the teacher who was a beloved father to them.

After Khayim's death, the author Dvora Omer wrote *Khavura u–shema alumim* (*A Group Named Youth*), whose content is the "Pedagogical Poem" of Israel.[5] Indeed, Khayim's life itself was a successful "pedagogical poem," rich in content and with a rhythm of its own.

Yeshayahu Kaspi (may his memory be for a blessing)

His death marked the departure of one of the stalwarts of the labor movement in general and the kibbutz movement in particular. He was born in Wysokie–Mazowieckie to religiously observant parents who were shopkeepers. They did not approve of their son's choices, when he decided to reject commerce and chose Zionist pioneering and farming, which led to a life of austerity and hard work. He emigrated to the Land of Israel in 1919, went to Hadera, and was overjoyed when he was hired as a shepherd. He later joined the communal settlement of Karkur, where he showed remarkable devotion and selflessness. He was also outstanding as a community guard, and risked his own life in times of emergency. His humanism led him to appreciate and like the Arab neighbors, who reciprocated his attitude. Thanks to this approach, he was able to reconcile bitter enemies and overcome obstacles.

[Page 147]

The basic element of his personality over the 44 years that he was in the country was his love of farming and his continual learning in all branches of agriculture. He was especially knowledgeable about farm animals, which he loved. He was a model farmer, hard–working and dedicated, and his achievements were impressive. In his last years, as a member of *moshav*Ganey–Am, he was awarded a prize for a high corn crop.[6] However, he was not motivated by a desire for prizes. He was totally devoted to the soil, and would happily recount his experience of a long day behind the plow, and the resulting long, straight furrow.

In fact, he loved directness and moral integrity in all areas of life; he suffered from the hypocrisy and corruption that were spreading in public life. He was as loyal to his views and tenets as he was to the simple life of a farmer.

Unfortunately, the last year of his life was marred by a struggle to retain his elementary right to work nationally owned land, after having done so for years and having improved his soil and production.[7] He was deeply offended by the very need for such a struggle, though high–ranking officials in the national corporations who knew him personally came to his defense. A letter of condolence sent by Avraham Hartzfeld to Yeshayahu's his brother, Dov (may he live long), stated, "He was a man of truth, and that is why I always supported him."[8] He really was a man of truth, for which he ceaselessly fought, and a man of the soil, which he worked and loved with all his heart. Symbolically, he collapsed and died at work in the field. May his memory be treasured among the towering, exemplary figures of the pioneers.

[Page 148]

Aryeh Viekha (may his memory be for a blessing), 1906–1974

We always called him "Leybele" affectionately, as he really was loved by everyone in our town. His home (with his wife Yaffa, may she live long) was open to friends and acquaintances. Many of us fondly remember his gracious hospitality and friendhsip during the first period of our lives in the Land of Israel; it was a difficult time of acclimation.

Aryeh was public–spirited; as a youth, he was already one of the organizers and activists among the young people of our town. He was instrumental in starting a branch of *HeHalutz* in Wysokie.[9]

His brother Eliyahu (a member of kibbutz Ashdot Ya'akov) recounts this interesting detail: "Te first local meeting of *HeHalutz* was in our home; the delegate from the central organization in Warsaw was Pinkhas Kozlovsky (Pinkhas Sapir)."[10]

Before emigrating to the Land of Israel, he trained as a carpenter with his future brother–in–law, Hersh Yitzkhak Trastenovitsh. His father, who recognized Aryeh's many gifts, did not approve of this plan, and tried to influence him to continue his *yeshiva* studies. (Like other observant Jews of the time, he aspired to have a son who would be a religious scholar and serve as a rabbi.) But Leybl stuck to his plan, and could think only of emigration. It was not long before his dream came true. He received an immigration certificate.[11] This was an important event in the town; a large crowd accompanied him to the Szepietowo train station for the start of his journey to the Land of Israel.

[Page 149]

Aryeh was the first in his large family to emigrate to the Land of Israel. His parents and sisters joined him there several years later. We remember his pleasure when they arrived; it was a pre–Holocaust rescue.

He emigrated in January, 1926, and settled in Hadera. Soon after he arrived he married Yaffa Trastenovitsh, who was from his home town. They created a warm, hospitable family.

Leybl joined the pioneering project whole–heartedly; in Hadera, at that time, the main goal was draining the swamps around the town. He became seriously ill with malaria, and the doctors advised him to leave the country in order to save his life. The very thought of leaving the country shocked him, and he did not follow their advice. He recovered, worked in orange orchards, and helped to establish Jewish laborers as the main work force. He later worked in carpentry, first with our Wysokie friend Shamay Kolodny, and then in a carpentry cooperative.

He soon joined the Haganah and was a member for as long as that organization existed.[12] When the bloody clashes of 1936–1939 broke out, he answered the call, left his regular work and relatively comfortable life, and became a Jewish guard in the British police force. Throughout his life, he was active in the Labor movement, and aided those in need.

* * *

He loved conversation, and had a fine sense of humor. His cheery laughter was often heard; he was never gloomy, even during difficult periods. Rather, he was always optimistic.

The last chapter of his life was bitter. He became ill with cancer, and struggled for his life in terrible pain for a long time. He died on March 31, 1974.

May he rest at peace in the soil of Hadera, the place he loved so much.

Translator's Footnotes:

1. Ben–Shemen is a youth village in central Israel, established in 1927. Its aim was to endow children with a Zionist ethic, teach them to work the land, and instill an appreciation of responsibility. The nickname "Khayim–from–heaven" rhymes in Hebrew: *Khayim min ha–shamayim.*
2. Berl Katznelson (1887–1944) was one of the intellectual founders of Labor Zionism and played a significant role in establishing the State of Israel. Yosef Khayim Brenner (1881–1921) was a Russian–born Hebrew–language author and one of the pioneers of modern Hebrew literature.
3. Siegfried Lehmann (1892–1958) was a Jewish educator who founded a Jewish orphanage in Berlin (1916) and opened an orphanage for Jewish war orphans in

Kaunas in 1919. He founded Ben–Shemen Youth Village in Mandate Palestine (1927) and directed it until 1957.

4. Moshe Smilansky (1874–1953) was a Zionist pioneer and farmer, as well as a prolific author of fiction and non–fiction literary works.
5. *The Pedagogical Poem* is the title of a book by Anton Makarenko, an influential educational theorist in the U.S.S.R., who developed the theory and methodology of upbringing in self–governing child collectives. One of these establishments was the Gorky Colony, the subject of the book, which was very popular in Israel in the 1950s.
6. A *moshav* is a cooperative agricultural community of individual farms.
7. Most of the land in Israel is owned by large national corporations such as the Jewish National Fund, with long–term leasing to individuals.
8. Avraham Hartzfeld (1888–1973) was an icon of the Labor Zionist movement, and a leading force in planning agricultural settlement in Palestine.
9. *HeHalutz* was a Jewish youth movement that trained young people for agricultural settlement in the Land of Israel.
10. Pinkhas Sapir was an Israeli politician during the first three decades following the country's founding. He held two important ministerial posts, Minister of Finance and Minister of Trade and Industry.
11. The British Mandate authorities strictly limited Jewish immigration to Palestine.
12. The Haganah was the main paramilitary organization of the Jewish population in Mandatory Palestine between 1920 and 1948.

Three who Fell

Translated by Yael Chaver

"Seeking my two friends, Eliyahu Grinshteyn and Yekhezkel Fridman." This brief message appeared in the Hebrew press in 1947. It was by Natan (Note) Krupinski, who was then in one of the postwar Displaced Persons camps in Europe.

Natan Krupinski (may his memory be for a blessing) immigrated to the Land of Israel in December, 1947, and was able to meet the good friends whom he had known since boyhood. Unfortunately, fate intervened, and the friendship between them did not last much longer; death in the near future awaited them all...

[Page 150]

The struggle against the Mandate authorities reached a peak in the months before the establishment of Israel.

Eliyahu Grinshteyn (may God avenge his blood) was murdered on February 25, 1948, by Arabs who ambushed him on his way to work, in the low–lying part of Haifa. He was 45.

Yekhezkel Fridman, on the other hand, was tragically killed by a Jew... He was a police guard in the British army camp at Sarafand, when a group of *Lehi* underground fighters attacked the camp in order to obtain weapons.[1] He was detained and ordered, along with two other guards, to face a wall. When he refused, turned and looked at the man who was detaining him with a cocked weapon, the latter shot him. He expired shortly afterwards...

He was 38 years old.

Our hearts ache to this day when we remember the terrible dramas that ended the lives of these three friends.

Eliyahu Meir Grinshteyn: head of the Wysokie Zionist organization. He was well-educated and very intelligent, and dedicated his talents, dynamic energy, and best years to Zionist activity. He had a great effect on the young people of Wysokie and on the Jewish community as a whole.

[Page 151]

He struggled to emigrate to the Land of Israel and finally reached it on April 5, 1935. He adjusted easily, married and started a family; but his happiness did not last. His life was cut too short.

* * *

Yehezkel Fridman (born in 1908), was Eliyahu's good friend and partner in all Zionist activities. He was insightful, and a lifelong optimist, whose wonderful sense of humor supported him in his hard life in Wysokie.

He survived the difficult sufferings of illegal immigration, including incarceration in the Cyprus detention camps.[2] He was finally able to realize his dream, and immigrated to the Land of Israel in 1938.[3]

The smiling man, who clung to his strong Zionist faith in spite of obstacles and bitter disapppointments in the country – was killed by a Jew, of all things…

[Page 152]

Natan Krupinski (may God avenge his blood) was also one of the Zionist activists in Wysokie. He married Fruma Brizman (may her memory be for a blessing) and lived in Wysokie up to the brink of the Holocaust. He survived all the horrors and tribulations that followed, and finally reached the Land of Israel at the end of 1947, full of suffering and bereavement...

He, who survived the Nazi hell, was killed a short time after he had reached the longed–for land.

The triple strand had now been severed forever...

―――――

Translator's Footnotes:

1. "Lehi" is the acronym for a Zionist paramilitary group 1920 and 1948, which often used terrorist methods in its actions.
2. The British government ran detention camps in Cyprus in 1946–1948 for the internment of Jews who had immigrated or attempted to immigrate to Mandate Palestine, in violation of British policy.
3. The text seems to be mistaken here.

―――――

[Page 153]

The Jewish Community of Wysokie–Mazowieckie

Translated by Yael Chaver

Seven kilometers from the railway line between Warsaw and Bialystok, not far from the murder field of Treblinka, the Jewish community of Wysokie–Mazowieckie existed for hundreds of years. It was founded by several families of Jewish farmers.

The Jews of Wysokie carried on their lives for centuries, and established a spiritual center within a small area; it included synagogue, house of study, *Talmud–Torah*, hostel, and poorhouse. These adjoined each other, and were surrounded by the Jewish cemetery. Only a few feet separated the eastern wall of the synagogue and the cemetery gravestones; the proximity of those praying with the world to come symbolized the terrible ending...

* * *

The small Jewish community did its best to separate itself from the Gentiles. An abyss lay between the Jewish community and the dozens of Polish villages in the vicinity, and a distrust stemming from the instinctive fear of the Gentile whose ingrained murderous tendencies might be revealed at any moment.

The incident of the *melamed* Rabbi Hershke is typical. One day he was traveling among fields and forests in a Gentile's cart. They had nothing in common, and sat silent almost the entire time, lost in their own thoughts. At the end of the journey, the Gentile addressed the Jew, "I could have murdered you the entire time we were alone on the road..."

This type of statement often turned into a shocking reality. The roads between Wysokie and Bialystok are soaked in Jewish blood, shed by their Polish neighbors.

* * *

The Brok stream, a tributary of the Bug river, separated the Jewish part of Wysokie from the Gentiles. The bridge over the stream, near the old cemetery, symbolized the geographic and ethnic boundary between both parts of the population.

There, at the bridge, stood the tall poplars whose twigs supplied the Jewish children with material for whistles, which they made after the Omer.[1] Jewish housewives dipped and purified dishes for Passover in the stream's water.

Near the bridge, leaning against the home of Berl–Khatzkel the baker, a narrow box full of metal wires stood upright. This marked the *eruv*, within which Jews could carry objects on Shabbes. The term was symbolic, as Jews mixed only with themselves in the Jewish courtyards, neighborhoods, and institutions that constituted the Jewish landscape of Wysokie.[2]

The *eruv* also symbolized the complete separation of the Jews from the Gentiles, who lived on the other side of the bridge.

———

Translator's Footnotes:

1. The 49 days between Passover and Shavu'ot are termed "the counting of the Omer," and are a time of semi–mourning, during which custom forbids haircuts, shaving, listening to instrumental music, conducting weddings and parties, and playing games.
2. The *eruv* (literally, mixing) is an urban area enclosed by a wire boundary that symbolically extends the private domain of Jewish households into public areas, permitting activities within it that are normally forbidden in public on the Sabbath.

The Holocaust

[Page 163]

During the Shoah

[Page 164]

Witnesses

The Jewish Historical Committee, Bialystok, September 12, 1945 L. G. 16

Under the Nazi Regime in Wysokie–Mazowieckie

by Natan Krupinski

Translated by Yael Chaver

(Provided by Natan Krupinski, born in 1905, lived in Wysokie–Mazowieckie before World War Two and during the Nazi occupation. Taken down by D. Kogan)

On the eve of World War Two, 500 Jewish families lived in Wysokie–Mazowieckie, numbering about 2,500 people. The town was taken by the Germans on September 10, 1939, and was promptly set on fire. They forced David Biadak to go back to his burning house, where he was incinerated alive.

All the Jewish men were herded into the church on September 12, and kept there for three days, with no food or water. Afterwards, they were sent to Zambrów. On the way, the exhausted Berl Vaynberg, Moyshe Grushko, Dov Balamut, and Gershon Friedman were shot and killed. Moyshe–Hirsh Kiviaku had a nervous breakdown and hurled himself into a well, where he drowned. Once they arrived at the Zambrów barracks, they had to file between rows of Germans, who beat them with sticks and tortured them. They were incarcerated in Zambrów only briefly, and then sent to Łomża. Some of the arrestees were able to escape from Łomża, and others were deported to Germany.

An order on September 19 forced all the Jews of Wysokie to leave the town by 3 p.m. of the next day. The Jews were frantic, having no idea where to run. They all fled with no possessions except for the clothes they wore; everything that had survived the earlier fire had been robbed by the Poles and the Germans. The Jews of Wysokie (except for the men who had been taken away earlier) ran to the nearby towns and to Bialystok.

On September 26, 1939, according to the Molotov–Ribbentrop pact, the Germans left eastern Poland, and Wysokie passed under Soviet authority.[1] The Jews expelled from Wysokie were able to return home, as did those who were deported to Germany. The Jew Sokhovolski was shot and killed by Germans on his way back to Wysokie.

The Soviet authorities helped the Jews of Wysokie to rebuild the burned town, and before too long it once again numbered 1,100 Jews.

On June 24, 1941, two days after the onset of the German–Soviet war, the Germans reoccupied Wysokie.[2] The second phase of their murderous regime began with the following decrees: all Jews had to wear a special insignia; kosher slaughtering was prohibited; Jews were forbidden to walk on the sidewalks; Jews were obligated to cut their beards; every morning,

[Page 165]

the Jews had to gather in the synagogue square, where they were beaten, abused and cursed. All, including women and children, were then taken for forced labor. Several Jews were arrested on the pretext that they were Communists. Among these were Shimon Tenenboym, who was publicly tortured to death. Shmuel Grinberg was deported to Bialystok, where he was shot to death.

On August 4, news came that the Germans had deported the Jews of the nearby cities and towns to an unknown destination.

On August 15, the *Judenrat* was ordered to have all the Jews assembled in the marketplace the next morning. Everyone panicked, as news from other locations had made clear the significance of this order. Many of the Jews fled from town.

On August 16, all the remaining Jews of Wysokie gathered in the market place at the designated time. The German commander, together with the Mayor and Chief of Police, selected several craftsmen from a prepared list; they were immediately released. The rest of the group were ordered to remain there, under heavy guard, until a sanitation committee would come from Łomża, supposedly in order to evaluate the health of the Jewish population.

The crowd of exhausted, desperate Jews was forced to wait for 24 hours. At 7 the next morning they were notified that the committee was unable to come due to traffic problems. It later emerged that the committee had been busy deporting Jews from other towns.

The first *Aktion,* and information that the Jews in ghettos would be safer, led the community leaders to request the establishment of a ghetto in Wysokie.[3] This was achieved after much effort.

On November 23, 1941, Jews from the nearby towns of Jablonka and Kulisz were sent to the ghetto in Wysokie. The ghetto now contained 1,350 Jews. Several days after its establishment, the Germans ordered them to pay a fine of 20,000 rubles. The fine was the revenge of the German commander for the fact that he had commandeered a pest–infested apartment in a building in a Polish neighborhood where Jews had never lived; he vented his anger by punishing the Jews.

There were no large–scale *Aktion*s in Wysokie for some time, but isolated Jews were victimized. On June 16, 1942, Leyb Wieszwa was arrested for buying an animal. He was sent to Łomża, and shot.

There were more and more rumors about ghettos that had been liquidated in the Warsaw area and elsewhere. These rumors were soon confirmed by refugees from various ghettos who fled to Wysokie. The sense of impending doom steadily increased in the ghetto. Five hundred Jews secretly left the ghetto. On the night of November 1, the ghetto was surrounded by Germans and Polish police. Wagons arrived shortly afterwards, and the Jews, who had been taken out of their houses, were "loaded" and deported to the labor camp at Zambrów.

[Page 166]

When the ghetto was terminated, the Germans and their Polish helpers collected all the sick Jews from their homes and the hospital, took them to one place, and shot them.

In this way, the Jewish community of Wysokie–Mazowieckie was exterminated.

The Jewish History Committee
M. Turk[4]
Chairman

Translator's Notes:

1. On August 23, 1939, Germany and the USSR signed a non–aggression pact (named for Russian Premier Molotov and German Foreign Minister who negotiated the agreement). The treaty defined the territorial spheres of influence that Germany and the USSR would have after a successful invasion of Poland.
2. The invasion of the USSR by Germany was intended to conquer the western Soviet Union so as to repopulate the area with Germans as well as to exploit oil reserves and agricultural resources.
3. *Aktion* was the German term for the mass roundup, deportation, and murder of Jews by the Nazis.
4. I was unable to translate the Hebrew abbreviation *mgr.*

———

[Pages 169-173]

The Historical Jewish Committee of Bialystok District
Bialystok, January 30, 1947

The Destruction of the Jewish Community in Visoka-Mozovietsk (Wysokie Mazowiecki)

(As testified by Avraham-Berl Sokol, 42 years old, a native of Visoka-Mozovietsk, who was in the concentration camps of Auschwitz, Mauthausen, Ebensee and Wels[1])

Translated from the Yiddish by M. Tork, Jewish Historical Committee chairperson for the Bialystok District

Translated from Hebrew into English by Uri Elzur

Donated by Dalia Taft

On June 22nd 1941, at 2am the Germans attacked the USSR. The next day our little town was already in the hands of the Nazis, and all the Jews of Visoka and Yablonka were ordered to work on the roads and to carve out stones under the supervision of German citizens equipped with clubs.

In August 1941 the Ghetto of Visoka was set up and Jews from the nearby small towns of Yablonka-Koscielna, Kulesze-Koscielna, Visung (Wyszonki?), Dabrowa and other were brought in as well. These Jews (2,000 people) were stuffed into the three ghetto streets, cordoned off with barbed wire. The ghetto had four gates that initially were guarded by Jewish police and later by Poles. Every day, the ghetto residents were taken out to work on the roads and after a 12 hour workday, each received 200 grams [7 ozs.] of bread and diluted soup or coffee.

Using different tricks I was able to sneak out to get food for my family – my wife and four kids[2], my brother and his family (living in Visoka) and my parents[3] (staying in the Zambrow camp). This went on until September of 1942.

On September 1st the Germans were looking for me in order to kill me for selling my horse. I knew I had to flee the ghetto. Three of my children (the older ones) wanted to join me, but I took with me only my son Moshele-Chaim, 12 years old. In the village (where I was hiding) the rumor that the Germans had ordered 600 wagons to get the Jews out of the Visoka Ghetto had spread. From afar I was able to see the bicycles rushing towards Visoka to surround the ghetto and prevent Jews from escaping.

The next day, on November 2nd, in the morning, the Germans, assisted by the Jewish officers, had kicked the people out of their homes, had badly beaten them and the crying and yelling were sky high. Many managed to run away to the forests and fields. But the cold and frost, hunger and persecution by the locals made it unbearable and many turned themselves into the Germans.

On November 7th I decided to go to Visoka, to my house, and get some belongings to take with me. Polish officers noticed me and informed the German Gendarmerie, who caught me, beat me until I was bloody and jailed me. I found Berka Shorshevitz (a Visoka resident) there, over 70 years old, who was hiding in the forest for some time, and had returned to Visoka and turned himself into the Germans. Within two days the jail was full of men, women, children and elderly people who chose to turn themselves in instead of dying out in the cold. From the Visoka jail, the Jews were transferred to the Zambrow Camp. They walked 19 kilometers (~ 12 miles) by foot, hungry and freezing,controlled by wooden clubs and dogs. On January 10th, 1943 the Zambrow camp was closed down and the Jews were sent to Auschwitz. From that time on, every Jew caught was shot and before his death was forced to dig his own grave.

A Christian from the Dabrowa-Koscielna village told me that after the Zambrow camp was closed, 14 Jews were captured. They brought them to the Jewish cemetery and ordered them to dig a big grave. They were all shot on spot. Among them were Ezra Lev, his wife and son ("sha'an" or watch maker), two sisters (from the Wilamovski family) and their children. When they were walking towards the cemetery one girl approached an officer and said: "Mr. Yaroshevitz, you have children yourself, do not kill us."

Yosel Zevische, a butcher from Visoka, hung himself with a towel in the Gendarmerie cell. Yankel Verobel (the tailor), his wife and child Yoelke-Itzele were hiding in the Falazi village. He was working for the farmers. The Gendarmerie found out. They caught him, put him on a wagon and brought him to a field not too far from Dabrowa-Koscielna, gave him a shovel and told him to dig a hole. He noticed they were about to kill him, so he threw the shovel at the feet of the Gendarmerie officer and started running away. They caught him and after cruel torturing they cut his body into pieces and buried him with his wife and son in one grave.

Zalman Susne of Visoka hung himself after staying in an attic at Stack village for some time. In the Schianzki village close to Yablonka, two Jewish families were hiding: Zlata and Motel Segal and Moshe Vizikevitch and his wife. They were informed on and the Polovka (field Gendarmerie) got to their hideout, ordered them out and [ordered them to] undress. They were made to stand by a wall while naked and were shot dead.

In the Stadrove village (near Yablonka) they found, towards the end of 1943, Kayla and Mordechai Segal. They were taken down from the attic where they were hiding and were shot. They left behind a six month old baby girl. A Christian women took the baby to her house and raised her. She is with the girl at Alek. She refuses to return the girl. She wants to immigrate to America.

Hazkel Segal and Moshe Vireszva are buried near the village of Falk.

Kadish Kojul and his niece Manes are buried in the Rambik forest. Not too far away from the forest Motel Nachman Segal's brother is buried.

In 1944, two weeks before the liberation, my brother Yeshayahu-Itzchak, his wife Faigel, their daughter Sara, 19 years old, and their son Avramaleh, 9 years old, were murdered.

Translator's Notes:

1. Ebensee and Wels were subcamps of Mauthausen
2. Wife Rivka and children Moshe Chaim (b. 1930), Yitchok Dovid (b. 1934), Roza Batia and Menachem (b. June 1941)
3. Shmuel Arye Sokol and Freidel (Rumnonick) Sokol

———

[Pages 174-183]

The Historical Jewish Committee of Bialystok District
Bialystok, February 2, 1947

What I Experienced at the Zambrow Concentration Camp[1] and Other Concentration Camps

(Testimony collected from Avraham-Berl Sokol, 42 years old, a native of Visoka-Mozovietsk,
who was in the concentration camps of Auschwitz, Mauthausen, Ebensee and Wels)

Translated from the Yiddish by M. Tork, Jewish Historical Committee chairperson for the Bialystok District

Translated from Hebrew into English by Uri Elzur

Donated by Dalia Taft

The Zambrow Camp had 17,500 Jews. The young prisoners were digging holes in the ground not knowing who they were destined for. The conditions were very harsh. Food was limited to a two pound loaf of bread made of bran and chestnut flour for 12 people a day, and a half liter [16 ozs.] of soup made of rotten potatoes with no salt. In the morning it was rare for anyone to get any warm water. Twice a day the Gendarmerie officers, with help from the Jewish police, who had a banner on their sleeves reading "supervision," would kick the people out of their barracks ("blocks") to stand naked and barefoot for two hours outside. Due to the cold, their faces swelled and became yellow.

Initially, they separated children from their parents. The outcry was sky high and the horror was so bad that they had to return the children to their parents.

The daily death toll in the camp was 100 people, mainly old people and childrens. The camp was divided into seven barracks. The human density was unbearable. Fourteen people had to sleep on bunks designed for six. There were cases where mothers killed their children out of desperation.

My family was 17 souls. When I was unable to see the suffering of my children and parents, I managed, using nepotism, to work in the kitchen for a few days. I worked from 4AM to 7PM. I had to carry water and ensure that the kitchen was clean. The Camp manager Block inspected the kitchen and was very pleased with my work. The next day they wanted to replace me with someone else, but the person in charge of the kitchen, Pesach Skabronk, claimed "If you remove Sokol from the kitchen, we'll be doomed." Thanks to him I was able to stay in the kitchen until the camp was closed. For my work I received three liters of soup. Any food I could get like beets, radishes, potatoes, etc. I brought to my family. My wife used to give to the children first and take the remains for herself. When the Germans and the Jewish police were not looking, we would collect the potato skins mixed with sand and cook them.

When the Zambrow camp was done with, they separated the old, sick and children from the rest of the population, about 800 people; that is, anyone who was not able to walk with the transport, and moved them to a specific "block," the hospital. In the last days, the Germans Bloch and Shandler and Dr. Knot (of Lomza) administered some medicine to the sick – a teaspoon of poison – and they all perished. They were buried in Zambrow next to the Russian cemetery. Many dead people were left on the bunks. I was removed from Zambrow on January 15th 1943. They brought us to Chizev (Tshizeva?) on farmer's wagons. It was extremely cold outside and on the way to the railway station 120 people froze to death. Many who disembarked from the wagons to the road to take care of their biological needs froze to death on the spot from the cold and from being weak.

As I was running after the wagon to take care of my children, I suffered more than once from being hit by the Germans' clubs, till I saw stars. The sleigh my wife and my elderly mother were riding in had turned over and they fell into the snow. My wife told me "If it wasn't for you I would be free from the trip to Auschwitz and could remain buried under the snow." I picked up the sleigh, put my children and aged mother in it and the trip continued. It was so freezing cold that the children were not able to cry anymore. We rode the whole night and traveled 22 kilometers (14 miles). My mother moaned "I wish I was staying at Zambrow."

At the Chizev railway station there was lots of fuss. The Germans were hitting the Jews on the head with clubs and forcing them to go into the cars. I wanted to save my family from the beating and rushed them into the cars. These were horse [cattle] cars and they stuffed ten [?] people into each of them, locked them and installed barbed wires around them and without food or water we were transferred to Auschwitz.

On January 17th 1943 we were brought to Auschwitz, to the "Judenrampe." When the car doors were open, the S.S. people with clubs in their hands were standing there shouting "Raus!" (Out!). The S.S. doctor was selecting people with his bamboo stick in hand, male and female separately. The males that were deemed not fit to work, and woman and children were put into the black cars (cars of death) that drove them off not too far from the gas chambers. They were ordered to undress and angry dogs attacked them, tore their flesh and chased them into the gas chambers. They stuffed up to 2,000 people into the two chambers, and if more people were still available they threw them on top of those standing inside. After 10 minutes of death throes, death had saved them of their misery. With gas masks on their faces, the S.S. people hermetically locked the doors, screwed them tightly, and placed a ladder three meters [10 ft.] high, where a porthole (small window) was located. With a hammer they hit a valve/cover and the gas (in the form of a dry grey powder) poured over peoples' heads. The screaming heard for kilometers died away after 10 minutes. Dead silence. A special company opened the door, dragged the dead bodies out and put them on a wheelbarrow – 30 bodies on each wheelbarrow – and carried them away to the pits. There they laid the corpses layer by layer on some branches and the Lieutenant Commander Steinberg[2] poured gasoline on them and lit the fire from four sides by himself. While doing it, he used to say "The burning Jews are the headquarters of the heavens." In each fire 2,500 corpses were burned. Outside of the camp there were three big pits. In two of them they burned the dead and in the third one they raked away the warm ashes and carried them away on wagons to the field or threw them into the Wisla river. After the corpses were removed from the gas chambers, the "barbers" would cut the women's hair and the "teeth pullers" would remove any gold teeth from the dead people's mouths.

In one case a beautiful French woman was hiding in a pile of goods. They noticed her after the whole group had been suffocated to death in the gas chambers. She pleaded with Lieutenant Commander Steinberg "I'm young, beautiful, I'd like to work, leave me alive." "Get dressed," the German told her and as she turned around to take her clothes, he shot her in the back.

The S.S. commander Moll[3] said "All the Jews of Lodz came to my factory" and indeed under his orders 60,000 Jews from Lodz were killed.

My wife was burned on January 17th, 1943 together with 16,000 Jews of Zambrow in the pits of Section Number Two.

The men that remained on the "Ramp" were divided into two groups, one on the right and one on the left. I was among the group on the left, not knowing what my fate was going to be. As I was standing in the lines of five, my son Moshele-Chaim jumped in front of me and said "Daddy, I want to be with you." He was bleeding and had lost the bread in his backpack. "Where is the bread?" I asked him. "A German beat me with a stick, and as I suffered that blow, I lost the bread." For three days he had not eaten. "Daddy, I still have one slice of bread." I snuck him into my line. He was shaking out of fear. As soon as the camp doctor saw him standing in line, he shouted "Heraus!" (Outside!). Like a bird the child flew out of the line and I have not seen him again since. From afar I saw my second son Itzele, nine years old, putting snow into his mouth in an effort to stop his hunger. I also saw my 70 year old mother with her eyes closed. Two women supported her with their arms. When my wife saw me from afar, she didn't care about the beatings the Germans gave her [for stepping out of line] and with my eighteen month old son Menachemke in her arms, she ran to me to say her farewell. "Forgive me" she said with the remaining strength she had, knowing death was close, and returned to her place. I was frozen like a fossil. They walked me to the camp. This is how my family was lost in twenty minutes, a blink of an eye.

They brought us to Block 20, beating us continually. After some time they took our clothes and we were ordered to stay outside in the biting frost (January 18th, 1943) for several hours. Many froze to death in the deep cold. Then they brought us to the bathroom and tattooed a number on the left hand. My number was 88966. For them I was not a human being but a number. When they yelled at me to get beaten, they were not calling my name but my number. The Jewish "Capo" – Merva of Makov (?) – trying to please the Germans, ordered me to "bend down" and with a thick stick he beat me very hard. This is the way we lived – hunger, fear, cold and beatings were our daily treats. Many signed up to Block 7 at their will, the block of death. This was the block they used to take people to the gas chambers, this is how we were shaking (?) in the claws of death and we were hoping.

On January 18th 1945 in the evening they took us out of the camp and made us run to Austria through Czechoslovakia. It was freezing cold and the snow reached our hips. 50% of us, who had no strength left to walk, died on the road. In Czechoslovakia they brought us to train cars, one hundred people in a car, and brought us to Austria, to camp Mauthausen.

On January 26th, 1945, they cut our hair. They took our clothes and left us naked. A new death camp; here the situation was worse than in Auschwitz. We were catalogued again; I got the number 120298 carved in tin. For two weeks we were there in cold and hunger. They forced us to stand outside for a whole day freezing with only our underwear covering our flesh. The body turned blue from the cold and tents of people were dying every day.

After two weeks they were ordered to give us striped clothes (like prisoners) and to move us to a new camp, Ebensee[4] in Austria. Here we worked in the forest, digging tunnels out of the mountain rocks and building warehouses. The situation at Ebensee was worse than the two previous camps. Nine people received an 800 gram loaf of bread a day, and one potato skin soup bowl was dealt to ten people. We ate in turns. We were standing in a circle and one by one each got one spoon of the soup. Once I got extra bread and margarine for my work. I sold it for a pair of shoes; otherwise my bare feet would have frozen.

We spent three winter months at Ebensee, working on stone mining, with our feet in water, under very harsh conditions and hunger and cold. Then they selected one thousand of us, myself included, to be transferred to camp Wels, where we labored fixing train rails that the Russians had dismantled. On our way to work and back and during work we were badly beaten. Twice a day we received a quarter liter of soup and a one hundred gram [piece of] bread. After four weeks of labor only 300 people remained of the 1000. As the war front got closer to Austria, the red army on one side and the American army on the other, they moved us back to Ebensee.

At Ebensee, our suffering had reached its peak; I ate live worms, soft coals, nibbled on bones, and chewed-up bitter grass (called "malitz," used to feed pigs) to fill out my stomach. My legs became swollen; I had my skeleton only. With my last strength I was able to hold out until May 6th, Liberation Day by the Americans. I am confident that were the Americans late by three to four days, I would not have testified here in front of you.

Three months after liberation, people were still running around naked, with swollen legs, covered with wounds, enraged in madness, unstoppable out of happiness.

Immediately, as the Americans entered the camp, they ordered the local Germans to remove three thousands corpses that the Germans did not have a chance to cremate and bring them to burial: Jews, Poles and Russians separately. The Jews' burial places were marked with a Magen David – the Star of David. This cemetery is by the Ebensee camp in Austria.

All hospitals were crowded with camp survivors. All were sick, exhausted, had intestinal and stomach ailments from the eating rush they suffered after the liberation. I was sick too.

Going through Austria, Czechoslovakia, and Upper Silesia[5], I got back to my hometown of Visoka Mozovietsk. On August 1st 1945, my feet were again on Visoka's ground. Out of my family of twenty, and from closer and more remote relatives – another thirty – I alone remained.

On November 2nd 1942, I was taken from Visoka and on August 1st 1945 I returned there. Two years and two days I was in Auschwitz. When I came to my hometown I saw the destruction that the Germans with their Polish aides had done to us. I also found the Gentile "goy" that lead me to the death camp. I went to the place where my house used to stand, to the place where my kids used to play, I went to the places where my brother's house used to stand. It had all been turned into desolation. I was told that my brother Ishayah-Itzchak and his family were killed two weeks before the liberation. I was left alone with no family or relatives.

Translator's Notes:

1. Zambrow was actually a ghetto but conditions were so bad it was initially called a concentration camp
2. SS officer Karl-Fritz Steinberg was in charge of Crematoria II and III in Birkenau
3. Otto Moll waa the Auschwitz crematorium chief
4. Ebensee is considered to be one of the worst concentration camps ever built
5. Upper Silesia is an area between Czechoslovakia and Poland

———

[Page 185]

The Zambrów Camp

Jewish Provincial Historical Commission, Bialystok, September 14, 1945 ; L.N. 67

Translated by Yael Chaver

(Presented by Mazur, who was born in 1899, lived in Wysokie–Mazowieckie before the war and during the German occupation, and was in the Zambrów labor camp. He survived in the forests around Wysokie–Mazowieckie. Protocol written by D. Kagan)

The camp was established on November 2, 1942, and existed until January 11, 1943. It contained 14,000 Jews who were collected from the entire region. People were not sent to hard labor, but the Germans contrived various ways to torture the prisoners. One of the worst chores was the daily "strolls." Regardless of the weather, all the Jews in the camp, including the old, the sick, and small children, were forced to take the terrible "strolls," naked and barefoot. During these murderous "entertainments," the weak succumbed. The food rations were appalling: it was almost impossible to survive on 150 grams of bread and half a liter of water daily. People went to any lengths to obtain a piece of bread. Those who were caught at this crime were severely punished by 25 or 50 whippings. Only death released these people from the horrible torture. Thirty deaths a day were common in the Zambrów camp. These conditions continued for two and a half months, when preparations began to transfer the Jews to a different camp; the camp commander promised that it would be a labor camp. To this end, all the craftsmen were registered, supposedly to work in the new camp.

The relocation of the Jews from the Zambrów camp in Oswiecim took place during January 11–17, 1943. All the women, children, elderly, and those who were feeble were gassed on the day of their arrival and were incinerated in the crematorium. Over time, the men were murdered by "selections" in which the weak were sent to the gas chambers.

This horrific news was brought by the Wysokie resident Sokol, who succeeded in surviving the hell of Oswiecim.

Evidence by Yellin, Chairman of the Jewish Provincial Historical Commission, headed by M. Turek

———

[Page 186]

Evidence

by Zelda Katsarevitsh

Translated by Yael Chaver

(Presented by B. Fuks, on behalf of the Historical Commission of the Bialystok region, headed by M. Turek, on January 26, 1947)

Zelda Katsarevich was born in Wysokie–Mazowieckie in 1906, and lived there until World War II. During the Nazi occupation, she and her three children managed to hide in the Wysokie forests for a long period of time. When she submitted this evidence, she was living in Biała Podlaska.

Zelda recounts that the Pole Iwonicki (aged 55) and his son–in–law Jan Ruszkowski (aged 24), residents of Jabłonka–Dobka village (in the municipality of Piekuta, Wysokie–Mazowieckie county), collaborated with the Germans during the occupation. Jan Ruszkowski was also a Gestapo agent.

After the liquidation of the Wysokie ghetto, she and her children – a girl of 12, a girl of 8, and a boy of 6 – went from village to village in search of refuge.

In April 1943, she and her children were hiding in Jabłonka–Dobka, in the hayloft of the peasant Iwonicki. Early that morning, one of the children fell ill and could not continue walking; she therefore decided to spend the day in the hayloft and leave at night. All four burrowed into the hay.

After some time, Iwonicki came in but did not notice them. Later, his son–in–law came to take hay for the animals, and discovered the mother and her three children. He immediately closed the door. The mother wept and begged him to let them stay in the granary until nightfall, or let them leave immediately. Ruszkowski responded, " I've already killed many young Jews and Jewish women; you and your children will also not escape me."

He left the barn and locked the door from the outside. He then went to the village elder and requested a wagon. The latter refused, saying that all the wagons were in the fields and in use by the laborers.

Ruszkowski and Iwonicki took the unfortunate mother and all three children into a room with broken windows. As one child was ill, the mother did not try to escape through the window frames but persuaded her 12–year–old daughter to jump out, thinking she might be saved. The girl jumped. However, Ruszkowski noticed her, and brought her back to the room after beating her severely. He now brought his own wagon. When the mother adamantly refused to get on, Ruszkowski and Iwonicki beat them savagely.

The murderers brought the mother and children to Piekut and turned them in to the German gendarmerie. They were then thrown into a cellar, where they remained all day. In the evening, two gendarmes and two men in civilian clothes took them out of the cellar and led them to a grove two kilometers from the village. Once they were in the middle of the grove, all four were shot in the back. The mother and her children collapsed on the spot.

[Page 187]

The mother's injury was not life–threatening, and she only fainted. When she opened her eyes she saw that the Germans were still there, and immediately shut her eyes. One of the Germans came near and shined a flashlight on her face. She held her breath, so that he wouldn't notice she was alive. She was bleeding all over. The sick child, whom she had kept with her while they were going to the grove, lay at her side. All four were tied with kerchiefs. The German tore off the kerchiefs and muttered, *Die Juden sind todt* (the Jews are dead).

When the Germans left the killing ground, Zelda gathered her strength and went to check on the children. She touched them and realized that they were all dead. She couldn't move from the spot for hours, but sat near the beloved bodies, wailing quietly. She finally parted from them and with her last shreds of strength made her way to Jabłonka, to the house of the priest, Kruszkowski, who had helped her several times previously. He was kind this time as well, took her in, and hid her. She lay unconscious for eight days.

The priest hid her for two months, until her injuries healed a bit. She then went to the village of Zarzyski; she found refuge for six months with the peasant Drangowski.

In November 1943, she returned to the forest, where she found other Jews from Wysokie. Zelda hid in the forest until Liberation.

———

[Page 189]

The Destruction of Wysokie

Evidence given by Yaffa Rozenberg, Leah Zolotolov, and Reyzl Vaynberg

Translated by Yael Chaver

I

Four days before Rosh Hashana, 1939, the Germans entered Wysokie. The entire town was burned down after a fierce battle between the German and Polish armies near the village of Goląsza. During the battle the residents hid in the deep trenches on the landowner's property. The first shots rang out at 2 p.m., and by 5 p.m. the town was in flames. As the Germans were overrunning the town, they threw a Molotov cocktail into each house. Those in the trenches witnessed a terrifying scene: the entire town was burning. Plumes of fire rose to the sky on all sides. People spent the night in the fields. In the morning, the Germans gathered all the men over age 17, and assembled them in the church, which had escaped the flames and was intact. The Germans displayed cruelty towards the Jews from the outset. That first day, Avraham Moshe Balamut and his son Berl were murdered. About 200 Jews spent two days in the church, with no food or drink. The other men managed to escape and found various hiding places. The women and children roamed the fields and the town's ruins.

[Page 190]

Those in the church were taken out two days later (including some Poles), and sent to the barracks at Zambrów. The Germans switched off the lights in the barracks so that the new arrivals would fall into the vast open cellars as they walked in. Several were killed in this manner. Some of the arrestees were taken to Stawiski and placed in the church. The next day, they were taken to Lyck, near Koenigsberg, where they were imprisoned for 24 hours. Many Jews from other towns were already in Lyck. From there, they were taken to Schtablak 2, where they were kept for two weeks. The Poles in the camp abused the Jews and removed their clothes. A few weeks later, the arrested Jews from Wysokie were returned to the town.

They found about 20 families in the destroyed town. These lived in the Kapitovsky house, the Segal house, the *Tarbut* school, and the Skavronek house. The Russians had already entered the town by this time. Many families also found refuge in the villages of Miesta and Vloysta.[1] The Russians did their best to house the Jews in peasant homes; those who wanted to rebuild their homes were given some construction materials.

The following families were able to rebuild their homes: Leyzer Yellin, Shmuel–Nachman Blumshteyn, Ayzik and Shlomo Zolotolov, Zbitse the butcher, Trastenovitsh the carpenter, Khayim–Velvl Wiecha, Avraham Herts, Meir Zolotolov, Lima Goldman, Alter Zak, Yehuda Zakomovitsh, Yitzkhak Vayzenberg, and Shmuel–Ayzik Yellin. The burned synagogue was not rebuilt, and the Jews gathered in private homes for prayers. Shmuel Grinberg was the residents' representative to the Soviet authorities. Once the Soviet regime stabilized, the craftsmen resumed their occupations. Some people found employment with the new regime, and many were storekeepers. The Russians also established a school for the Jewish children, but the teachers and educators were not Jewish. The young people were drafted into the Russian army, and some were pressed into building defenses. Most of those who worked at the defenses stayed in the town. At the outbreak of the Russo–German war, the Nazis quickly conquered eastern Poland, and the Russian army hastily retreated. Some of the Wysokie residents left the town along with the Russians.

II

On July 22, 1941, the first day of the German offensive, the Luftwaffe bombed the Russian airport in Wysokie. The next day, July 23, the Germans came to Wysokie from Zambrów. As they arrived, they promised the Jews' representative that they would not be harmed. For a few days, there was no authority in the town. Zaremba continued as mayor, and the Jews asked him to restore some order to the lawless town. At that transitional time, Rabbi Alter Zak was very active, and organized vital activities to ensure the townspeople of elementary services.

[Page 191]

A few weeks later, the Jews asked the Germans to establish a ghetto in their neighborhood, as protection from the rampaging Gentiles. The Germans agreed, and the ghetto soon extended from Yakobi's house to Bielski's house, the location of the main gate. The fence continued along Mistka Street, between the houses of Vrubel, the cobbler, and Aharon Leyzer, the carpenter. This was the location of the second gate. The fence surrounded the entire market square. The third gate was on the "Hoyfishe Gas," near the butcher shops. The old cemetery was inside the ghetto. The fourth gate was near the bridge of Mordechai, the blacksmith. The left side of the "Hinter Gas" was inside the ghetto, and the right side was outside it.[2] The ghetto was established a few days before Yom Kippur. Christians who lived inside the ghetto exchanged houses with the Jews who lived outside it. The few Germans in the town (about ten) were quartered in the Kapitovski house, on the Szepietowo road.

At its establishment, the ghetto housed about 2000 people. This included Jews from the surrounding villages of Kulish, Jablonka, Dąbrowa, Vishang, Pingot, and Tatara.[3] The German authorities ordered the Jews to elect a 13–member *Judenrat*. The members were Rabbi Alter Zak (Chairman), Avraham Herts, Fishl Segal, Meir Mayzner, Betsalel Tenenboym, Hersh–Yitzkhak Trastonovitsh, David Mazur, Eliyahu Vansover, Barnholts, Pesach Skovronek. Ya'akov Melnik, Shmuel–Ayzik Yellin, Tankhum of Kulish, and Chava Yellin as secretary.

All Jewish men and women over 15–16 were forced to wear a yellow patch on their outer clothing, front and back. At first, they also had to wear a yellow band on one sleeve.

Rabbi Alter Zak and Avraham Herts (who was fluent in German) represented the ghetto. Avraham Herts died in the ghetto in the late summer of 1942, and was eulogized by Rabbi Alter Zak. He was buried in the Jewish cemetery outside the ghetto.

How did the Jews in the ghetto make a living? Two oil presses were opened, one at the house of Ayzik Krupinski and the other at the house of Efrayim Shtern, the carpenter. According to orders, the ghetto had to supply about 250 laborers daily for road–building and tree–felling in the forest. Jews were hired during the harvest season, to gather the crops on the landowner's property in Szepietowo, in exchange for fresh produce. Craftsmen (cobblers, tailors, furriers, carpenters, tinsmiths, and others) would go to the villages to practice their trades, using permits the villagers obtained from the Germans. They would buy goods and sell them to the villagers in return for fresh produce. The Germans established a Jewish militia in the ghetto. Among its members were Shmuelke Sosna, Hershl Zilberfenig, and Pesach Dalangvitsh. Moshe Brenner and Yudl Zak were appointed commanders. There was no electrical lighting in the ghetto; kerosene and candles were used throughout its existence.

[Page 192]

III

One evening in the late summer of 1941, German gendarmes appeared in the ghetto, announcing that at 7 a.m. the next morning all the ghetto inhabitants had to gather on the square of the Polish school. Everyone appeared the next morning. The men were sent to various tasks, while the women and children returned to the ghetto.

That day, refugees from the region (Czeszów, Tykocin, Rotka, Zarumb, and Zambrów) came to Wysokie. They told us that the Jews there had been rounded up and shot dead, and the bodies had been flung into pits dug earlier. Everyone was terrified, and began thinking of ways to avoid this fate. Rabbi Alter Zak went to see the landowners around Szepietowo, Szczeczin, and elsewhere, and asked them to take young Jews as laborers on their properties. Once they agreed, all the young people over age 17 left to work on the estates. Each group of fifty included a cobbler (a highly desirable profession).

The youthful energies of the young people found an outlet in singing and dancing every Sunday; it was so infectious that the Gentiles in the area would come to have fun with the Jews.

About a month later, there came another order to assemble. This time the young people did not obey. Instead, they fled to the nearby forests (Masuria, Szepietowo, etc.). Only the middle–aged and the elderly gathered in the market square. Nothing happened this time, either, but the women were ordered to weed out the grasses between the square's cobblestones. A third order to assemble also proved to be a false alarm. Two people were sent to work at road–building between Ząbrowo and the Tykocin junction, near Bialystok. The Germans ordered the destruction of the old roads and the construction of asphalt pavement instead. Work in the quarries was primitive: no cranes were used to raise the rocks. Everything was done by hand: quarrying the stone, taking it up to the smasher, removing the gravel, etc. All the labor was forced, without pay. Food for the laborers was supplied by the *Judenrat*. The abusive German overseers could be bribed with boots, fabric, or meat, so that they wouldn't torture the workers. Craftsmen and others who made their living independently paid the *Judenrat* a ransom to be released from the forced labor. This eased the job of the *Judenrat*. This work continued up to the liquidation of the ghetto. People who were old, poor, and had no family, stayed in the firefighters' hall and subsisted on community funds. The *Judenrat* did its best to minimize the numbers of people concentrated in one place and made sure that some of the single persons would be taken into homes.

With the onset of winter, heat in homes became a necessity. The laborers chopped firewood from the roots of the thick trees in the Masurian forest. The wood was distributed by the *Judenrat*.

There were many examples of bravery and of people risking their lives in the ghetto. Especially noteworthy were the physician, Dr. Golda Zak, and Rabbi Alter Zak, chairman of the *Judenrat*. Dr. Golda worked long hours taking care of the sick and the feeble, free of charge. She worked to the limits of her strength during the cold winter nights.

[Page 193]

Dr. Golda Zak
(may God avenge her blood)

Rabbi Alter Zak
(may God avenge his blood)

Rabbi Alter Zak also risked his life often, proudly and bravely confronting the Germans in order to save Jews. Once, when the sirens sounded and most people fled, Rabbi Alter remained alone in the ghetto, except for his son Yudel.

IV

On Sunday, November 1, 1942, about 300 wagons arrived in Wysokie. The Germans said that they were meant to transport seedlings for new forests. A few hours later, many armed Gentiles began to congregate at the ghetto's fence. This seemed suspicious, and that evening some of the ghetto's residents fled to the forests. Naturally, no one slept that night, fearfully awaiting the next day.

At 4 a.m. the next morning, Monday, members of the *Judenrat* and German policemen went through the ghetto streets, ordering everyone out to the market square. Hundreds of Gentiles waited around the fence, anticipating the loot. Some of them laughed happily at the misfortune of the Jews about to be executed. Some time later, several hundred Germans appeared. The young people were working on the roads outside the ghetto at the time.

The Germans forbade the Jews to take anything with them, and ordered everyone onto the wagons. The Germans tried to calm the Jews, telling them that they were being taken to Ząbrowo, but no one believed them. Everyone knew that this was the last road. When the Jews arrived in Ząbrowo, they were ordered into houses that had already been designated for them. As noted, the young people were outside the ghetto that day, and did not know what was happening. Suddenly, that morning, the German foreman appeared. A few moments later, about twenty Germans, armed with rifles, came, and ordered the 40–50 laborers into a truck. None of the laborers escaped, as they were surrounded by Germans. They were taken to Rudki and imprisoned. Additional Jewish laborers from Wysokie were occasionally brought in. They stayed there from 8 a.m. until 2 p.m., when they were taken out of the prison, loaded onto wagons, and tied hand and foot with ropes; this operation was carried out by Poles. The convoy left Rudki for Zambrów, accompanied by an armed guard of Poles and Germans. As they traveled, the Germans spotted a few Jews on foot and began to chase them. The prisoners made good use of the situation, and managed to loosen the ropes with their teeth; about ten prisoners were able to escape. The Polish cart driver looked the other way, and the guys jumped off the wagons and ran to the village of Kuski, near the forest. The armed guardsmen shot at them, but missed.

[Page 194]

Those who escaped from the wagon included Leymke Plishka, Efrayim Mazur, Ayzik Sokal, and Ya'akov Tiktshinki. They hid in the forest all night and headed to Wysokie the next morning. Near the village of Galasza, they met Fishl Segal and his son, Pesakh. Leymke Plishka had a loaf of rye bread that he had received from a Gentile. The Christian Susaski, of Wysokie, reported that he gave Segal clothes. The first snow of the season fell that night, covering the fields. The next day, Motl Pianka met his parents in the forests near Wysokie–Wróble. They went on through the Masurian forest, where they met about 150 Jews. They dug bunkers and trenches under the trees in the forest, camouflaging them with a covering of branches. Days were spent lying in the forests. They emerged at night to buy food from the villagers. This went on for ten days.

In mid–November, the forest was surrounded by a company of German soldiers, with Polish helpers. They shot at the bunkers, and ordered everyone out. They shot Fishl Segal, David Guzovski. Avraham–Yitzchak Biedak, and Yente Shereshevski, who were all killed on the spot. Others were injured, and, due to lack of medical help, suffered for days until they died. The rest, about 120, were taken to Wysokie and kept all night in a crowded room where they could barely stand upright. They next day, they were taken to Zambrów on wagons. Their despair was so great that no one tried to escape. In Zambrów, they were kept in barracks, with no water, and one loaf of bread for eight people. Most of them fell ill with jaundice and dysentery; many died of disease and exhaustion.

They were kept in Zambrów until January 15, 1943. That night they were taken by wagons to Czyżew . By this point, their clothes had become rags; some were naked and barefoot. David Yakovnitser and others died en route of the cold.

In Czyżew, they were packed into rail horse cars, and taken to Auschwitz with no food. They managed to break open a door; Shmuel Sosna, Hershl Virubnik, Hershl Zilberfenig, Dalangevitsh, and Itsl Volmer (Vafnitsky's grandson) jumped out of the rushing train. Itsl Volmer was the only one who survived.

[Page 195]

They reached Auschwitz on January 17, 1943, and were greeted by severe blows. Some of the men were taken to forced labor. These included Leymke Plishka, Shlomo Zolotolov, Avraham Berl Sokal, Yisraelke Yellin, Ben Shilem, Yankl Dalangevitsh, Bendet Pianka, Avraham and Shlomo Tenenboym, Chayim Kaviar, Moshe Yosl Kasyar, Eliyahu Hershl Krupinski (son of Ayzik), Khayim Shaklo, Moshe Perlman, Shiyeh Segal, Yankl Zlodka, David Kiyek, Yeshayahu Vizenberg, Simkha–Velvl and Yehuda (Yudl) Zak, Meir Plishka, Hertzke Skvornek, Meir (son of David) Yakovtsiner, Pesakh Vaysbord, Shlomo Klodo, Hilel Shrenits, Khayim Velvl Wiecha, Simkha Sokal, Eliezer Hakhlovski, and Leyzer Khamilevski.[4] All the others – the elderly, women, and children – were taken to the gas chambers. The doors shut hermetically once people were inside, and they were then asphyxiated by gas introduced into the chamber through the window. The bodies were moved into pits, and covered in chlorine. Those who survived had their arms tattooed.

Life in Auschwitz resembled life in the barracks. Each person received ¼ kg bread daily, thin soup, coffee, a spoonful of jam, and cheese. The prisoners cleared forests, built roads, and did construction. Those who were too weak were shot or sent to the gas chambers. At the morning roll call, people were examined to see whether they were strong enough to work. Anyone who was infirm or sick was sent to the gas chambers. The few who survived stayed in Auschwitz until January 19, 1945. That day, they were marched to the concentration camp at Mauthausen, Austria, where they worked at digging tunnels. The food ration was steadily reduced from a daily 250 grams of bread to 70 grams. Conditions continued to deteriorate as the Allied powers approached.

Most of those who remained alive in spite of the hells they had undergone largely emigrated to Israel, and now live and work in the free State of Israel.

Translator's Notes:

1. I could not identify these villages.
2. The Yiddish *Hoyfishe Gas* and *Hinter Gas* mean, respectively, "Courtyard Street" and "Back Street."
3. I could not identify Kulish, Vishang, Pingot, and Tatara.
4. I have transliterated the names to the best of my ability.

Page 195]

Plowmen have plowed over my back...[1]

by Leymka Plishko (Giv'at Ha–Shlosha)

Translated by Yael Chaver

As early as the last days of August, 1939, we sensed that "something serious is about to happen." However, no one imagined that the "something" would mark the beginning of the terrible tragedy of the Jews of Europe.

I cannot describe all the stages of the destruction of Jewish Wysokie. Here, I would like only to describe the events that happened to me and that I witnessed.

The events are as fresh in my mind as though they happened yesterday. As I describe them, I seem to relive the horrors of that dark period, which is unparalleled in the bloody history of our people. Once again, I see the innocent victims writhing in pain, the bloodthirsty murderers shooting helpless women and children, the blood flowing unchecked...the gas chambers, the heaps of corpses, the tall crematorium smokestacks that spewed thick, black smoke day and night. Sometimes, I can still feel the stifling odor that meant only, "You are still alive now, but know that your turn will come, too, and soon the smoke rising from the smokestack will incorporate your incinerated body, will rise to the sky and be lost in the dense black welter."

[Page 196]

So it began

September 1, 1939.

Nazi Germany attacked Poland. World War II began. The town was struck by terror. The radio brought news of bombed towns, battles raging between the German and Polish armies. Everyone was fearful and panicked when word came that the German forces were advancing and the Polish army was retreating hastily. The river of fire was rapidly expanding, inundating towns and villages, and approaching our town.

Four days before Rosh Hashana, on September 10, 1939, German forces took Wysokie–Mazowieckie. The city became a rubble heap, after having been set on fire in previous bombings. But that was not enough for the Germans. They burned up the few structures that remained standing. That day, Jewish Wysokie suffered its first two victims: Avraham–Moshe Balamut and his son Berl were shot by the Germans, and Yudl Zilberfenig, who had gone to Wiszew the day before the war broke out to buy beer from the brewery, was killed in the bombing.

The Jews who had fled from the bombed town to the fields and towns between Wysokie and Mistka village, were safe for the moment. They found refuge in the towns of Sokoły, Ciechanowice, Zambrów, and even as far away as Bialystok.[2] My family – my father Hershl Plishko, my mother Feyge, my three brothers and four sisters – fled to Sokoły.

The day after the Germans arrived, they arrested almost one thousand men over the age of 17 (300 Jews and 700 Poles) and jailed them in the Catholic church. I was one of the arrestees. The older men – Jews and Poles – were freed the next day. The others, about 700 or 800, were deported: some to East Prussia, to Schtablak camp, and some to Zambrów, to military barracks that had been turned into an internment camp.

The transport to Zambrów, which consisted of 150–200 Jews, was forced to walk. En route, the exhausted Berl Vaynberg, Moshe Grushko, Berl Balamut, and Gershon Fridman, were shot.

At Schtablak, the Poles were placed in the barracks, whereas the thousands of Jews from the cities and towns of Brańsk, Zambrów, Łomża, Kolno, Śniadowo, Stawiski, and other places, were sent to the open field and given tents to set up. At night, the Poles attacked them, took the tents and pillaged them, and took the clothes of many people, leaving them naked and barefoot. Trying to avoid additional robbery, the Jews invented various stratagems: they wore a boot on one foot and a shoe on the other, and ripped their clothes so that they would not appeal to the Poles. Quite a few Jews successfully fought back the Poles.

[Page 197]

We stayed in Schtablak for two or three months, not working. We received one slice of bread a day and some water, and did not change clothes or underwear the entire time. Our days were largely spent picking out pests from our clothes... The tents were so crowded that people literally sat on each other. There was no room to lie down, and we slept sitting up. Some, who could not withstand the hunger and inhumane conditions, as well as the constant verbal abuse by the Germans and the Poles, went insane. Others died due to suffering and distress.

Eventually, we learned that people who had lived in areas taken, or "liberated" by the Russians (using Russian terminology) would be returned to their homes by the Germans. We were told that we would return to Wysokie–Mazowieckie, which – according to the "partition" – was under Soviet authority.[3]

We were stood in rows and led to the railroad station. Traveling in freight cars, we arrived in Ostrołęka. We marched through Ostrołęka to the strains of military music, and crossed the Narew river on foot (the bridge had been destroyed in the fighting). About two km out of Ostrołęka, we realized that no one was guarding us. We were walking through fields of mangold (chard), which we ate and took with us, we headed for Śniadowo. There were 70 or 80 of us from Wysokie. As we passed through peasant areas, we entered their courtyards, and snatched morsels of pig or chicken feed; even these crumbs were better than mangold.

In Śniadowo, we went to the house of the painter Blumshteyn's brother, whose son was among us. We were given food and water. After a short rest, we went on to Zambrów, which was under Russian control. The local Jews greeted us warmly and made sure that we received hot food. We later continued to Wysokie.

Wysokie, of course, had been burned to the ground when the Germans arrived, and its Jews had found refuge in nearby towns. We scattered to the towns in search of our families.

Under Soviet Rule

Our townspeople slowly started to return to Wysokie. Some settled in the few houses that remained standing after the fires, while some built cabins of wood sold by the Soviets at full price. Bit by bit, life embarked on a normal course.

Saturday night, June 21, 1941, the Polish school held a ball. The young people danced, while German aircraft flew over the town. The Russians reassured us, saying that these were only maneuvers; they quickly had to change their tune after the planes bombed the airport built by the Soviets near Wróbla forest. That was when they realized that Germany was attacking the Soviet Union.

[Page 198]

Many Jews fled to the forests and fields. The next day, June 23, the Germans were in Wysokie. They put up posters ordering the residents not to leave town, to be calm, and no one would be harmed. The "sincerity" of their promise was soon exposed. The day after they arrived, they arrested Shmuel Grinberg, who was chief of police under the Soviet authority, and had been treating the entire population – Jews and Poles alike – very fairly. As chief of police, he hid a rich peasant named Dolongovsky from Brika village in his house. When the Germans came, Grinberg asked the peasant to return the favor and hide him. The Polish peasant "remembered" his kindness, and turned him over to the Germans. Shimon Tenenboym was arrested at the same time. The Germans took them both to Zambrów, and murdered them there.

Under German Rule

The ghetto was established shortly after the Germans arrived. It was headed by the *Judenrat*, which represented the Jewish population and was responsible to the authorities. The Germans also set up a Jewish police force, which was tasked with keeping order within the ghetto. It should be noted that the Jewish police worked together with the *Judenrat*, which spared no effort; its members even risked their lives to help the Jewish residents.

The *Judenrat* had to supply the Germans with workers. The first job was scattering sand on the roadways. Some of the younger people worked for the landowners, and handed their compensation – potatoes and other produce – over to the *Judenrat*, which distributed the food to the Jewish population.

The *Judenrat* set up a soup kitchen. All the needy, especially refugees from nearby towns, received two hot meals daily. The *Judenrat* organized the work so that they could distribute food to Jews from nearby towns who were building the Bialystok–Warsaw and Tykocin roads. They risked their lives to help their needy brethren.

When winter began, the Germans sent young Jews to the forests to cut trees, chop them, and bring them in as firewood. As compensation, they were allowed to extract the tree roots for their own use. The Jewish workers handed them over to the *Judenrat*, which distributed them equally among all the ghetto residents, for heat and cooking purposes.

Transportation in the ghetto was reduced to two wagons and their horses. They served to transport the workers, to bring food to the road–builders (who were working 20–30 km from the town), and to bring food and firewood from the towns into the ghetto.

[Page 199]

The *Judenrat* was headed by Rabbi Alter Zak, who risked his life more than once, and saved many Jews thanks to his firm stance against the Germans. The Germans ignored his impertinence, for some reason, and never punished him. They may have had orders not to hurt the head of the *Judenrat* so as to avoid unrest among the Jews. The Jews were scheduled to be liquidated in stages, and it may have been too early to remove their leader.

Avraham Hertz was Rabbi Zak's closest helper in the *Judenrat*. He also served as liaison between the Germans and the *Judenrat*, and was in charge of handing over the quotas of gold, boots, and other goods imposed on the Jews. He cracked under the pressure, became ill, and died at the end of summer in 1942.

Conditions in the ghetto deteriorated steadily. The Jews lived in constant fear. When night fell, no Jew knew whether he would live to see morning. Terrible news about events elsewhere came constantly. Everyone felt that the tragic end was drawing near.

Liquidation of the Ghetto

On Sunday, November 1, 1942, I heard rumors that the Germans had ordered wagons in order to remove all the Jews from the ghetto. We younger men worked at building the road between Zambrów and Bialystok, about 35 km from Wysokie. We gathered to discuss our plans for the next day. The fateful question was, should we or should we not report for work in the morning. Despite our hesitation, we decided to report. Our main motivation was the knowledge that if we did not show up at work, the Jews of the ghetto would be punished.

That evening, Sunday night, Leyzer–Yosl arrived from the ghetto, with the wagon of food sent by the *Judenrat*. He confirmed the rumors that the Germans had ordered wagons to move out all the Jews in the ghetto.

The next day, when we reported to work, Schwartz (who was in charge of the camp) appeared, armed with a rifle. We were surprised, as he had not carried arms up to that point. His first question was whether anyone was missing. Before we could reply, we were surrounded by armed Germans. We were ordered onto trucks and taken to the town of Rudki, where we were locked up in the jail. This operation had been planned and executed with German precision. All the Jews from the nearby towns who had been working at road–building were also brought in. We were kept in the jail until the afternoon.

We were then loaded onto wagons, and our arms and legs were tied to the sides of the wagon to prevent any chance of flight. Forces of the Polish police and German *Gendarmerie*, armed with automatic rifles, accompanied us.[4] We knew that many Jews from Rudki and Zambrów had been murdered on this road. There was no doubt in our minds: it would be our last road. We decided to take every possible chance we could at escape. But how can one escape with ropes digging into one's arms and legs? Yet we were determined not to let them lead us like sheep to the slaughter.

[Page 200]

We started to gnaw at the ropes; they gradually loosened, and we wriggled free. But each of us stayed in place; we knew that if our overseer escorts noticed, we would be shot on the spot. This danger was very real, as each group of three wagons were accompanied by a fourth wagon carrying armed Germans and Polish policemen.

It was chance that enabled us to carry out our plan. As we approached the Kosoka forest, a young couple came up. The Germans asked them if they were Jewish; they immediately ran toward the forest. The guards opened fire. We made good use of the moments when the guards were distracted, jumping off the wagons and running as fast as we could toward the forest, to Chervony Bur. The guards shot at us from all sides, but the trees shielded us: no one was injured.

Ten of us in all – Yankl Tikoshinsky, Ayzik Sokol, Efrayim Mazur, a guy from Warsaw, and others whose names I don't remember – ran through the forest for several kilometers. When we were sure that no one was pursuing us, we lay down for a rest. After a while, we started to be hungry. However, we had nothing to eat, and lay there suffering. We spent the night in the forest; at dawn, we oriented ourselves, and decided to return to our area.

A peasant we met on the road asked us where we were going. When we replied, he said, "Do you want to die? Don't you know that the peasants are killing every Jew they find on the road? You'd be better off staying in the forest."

A shudder went through us. Death awaited us at every turn. If the Germans don't kill us, the Poles will. There's no escape. The world has conspired to kill us.

We split into small groups of two each, and returned to the forest to hide. We stayed until nightfall. By this time our hunger had become painful; we could barely move our legs. We decided to leave the forest and search for our loved ones. We had nothing to lose; we would die in any case if we stayed in the forest.

We walked alongside the road. When we reached the spot where the Germans had shot the young couple, we saw their corpses lying in the same place. Going through Kolaki forest, we continued through forested areas. Occasionally, we approached a shack, or a forest worker, and asked for bread. Dogs were set on us everywhere and we were driven away. The Poles received us with contempt and curses, shouting, "We have no bread for *zhids*. It's too bad that you weren't all killed!"

I entered the home of a peasant acquaintance. He was friendly, and invited us all into his home, gave us food and drink, as well as a large loaf of bread for the road. The moment we left his home, young Polish boys started to chase us. They planned to catch us and turn us over to the Germans. We scattered in every direction. Romek, from Warsaw, and I ran together. I held on to the loaf of bread, even though it was slowing me down.

We continued on our way. Early in the morning, as we were leaving the village of Galasza and nearing Wysokie, I noticed two people walking in the distance. They hid from us, and we hid from them. I realized they were Jewish. When I came near, I recognized Fishl Segal and his son Peysekh. When I asked for news from the town, Peseykh burst out in tears. Weeping, he told me that all the Jews had been taken out of the ghetto, and no one knew where they were. I placed the loaf of bread on the ground, saying, "What use are the tears? We are all lost. But as long as we can breathe, we must fight to stay alive. Let's sit down and eat."

[Page 201]

Fishl replied, "These days, one doesn't throw away bread. You were lucky to get a loaf, so guard it well. That loaf might save you from death."

I said, "On the contrary. During this difficult time, people must help each other. As long as I have a slice of bread, I will share it."

We sat on the ground and ate the bread, dampened with our tears.

We continued deeper into the Galasza forest, not knowing where to go or what to do. We were at our wits' end, no longer even afraid of death. Sitting in the forest, we saw someone approaching. I thought, "Let the inevitable happen. I can take no more." When he came nearer, I recognized him. It was the Pole Sosnowski, whom I had known a long time. He calmed us down, saying, "Don't be afraid. I will help you as much as I can. Stay here–I'll be back soon."

Sosnowski left. We though he would be back with a gang of Poles, or Germans. But, to our surprise, he returned alone, carrying food and cloths to bind up our bare feet. When we jumped off the wagon, my friend Romek threw away the shoes he was carrying, in order to run faster.

We said our goodbyes. Romek and I went to Wróbla , while Segal and Peysekh went another way. In a settlement near Wróbla, we met Motl Pianko. He told me that my parents were hiding in the forest, near the home of the peasant Wysocki. I went to that house. "That's right," he answered. "Your parents are not far away." I went searching, and found them.

It snowed heavily that night. We lay in the forest all night, barefoot and almost naked. The next day, I told my father that I was going to look for my brother Meir in the Masuria forest. And indeed, when I came to the forest I found the eight people who had fled when the Polish youths had attacked us.

Many Jews found refuge in that forest, and hid in shelters they had constructed. They numbered about 150, including the Segals. We would go out at night to seek food, and spend the day in the shelters. One day in mid–November, around noon, my brother Yisra'el came from the Wróbla forest, and tearfully told me that our parents had sent him to bring me food, but that they were gone when he returned. I calmed him, took him in and gave him some food. We were about to leave to look for our parents, when I saw the barrel of a machine–gun being inserted into the shelter. The German command was instantaneous: "Everyone out! I will open fire unless you come out."

[Page 202]

We crawled out of the shelter. I immediately saw that the forest was completely surrounded by Germans and armed Poles. Before I could grasp what was happening, an armed German walked up to Fishl Segal and shot him in the mouth. Then he went to Hersh–Yitskhok Trestanovitsh and did the same. Both men collapsed and died on the spot. After he had finished off the first two, he began shooting at all the Jews with his automatic weapon. Some were killed immediately, and many were wounded; many of the latter died in the forest. The rest, some with injuries, were ordered to line up, and were marched to Wysokie. We were taken to a stable, where we stayed all night. It was so crowded and airless that when the doors were opened in the morning, several people had suffocated. Leaving the stable, we felt as though we were emerging from a furnace. The chief of the *Gendarmerie* later came, brandishing a pistol, and started yelling and cursing: "You murderers, partisans, ruffians, were planning to annihilate us. However, we are letting you live, because we are good people. We are sending you to the labor camp at Zambrów." The wagons came a few moments later. We were loaded onto them, and taken to Zambrów.

We were depressed, exhausted, and hungry, sure that we were being taken to a place where our burial pits had been dug, or that we would be ordered to dig our own pits. However, this time we were wrong. We arrived in Zambrów, all still alive. Most of the Jews of Wysokie were here. The Germans divided us according to our places of origin. Each town had its own *Judenrat*. Once again, we found Rabbi Alter Zak and his daughter, the physician Golda Zak, as well as the other *Judenrat* members who did all they could to ease conditions for the unfortunate Jews. Once again, a soup kitchen was set up, and each loaf of bread was divided into eight portions. A bit of drinking water was handed out. There was no salt at all. Many died of disease and starvation.

The Germans took 2 or 3 people from each bloc, and sent them to the forest to gather twigs and make brooms, for the barracks floors. We would bribe our German escorts and, in between the bundles of twigs, smuggle in loaves of bread we bought from the peasants. One day, on December 31, 1942, the Germans ordered us to lay down the bundles of twigs, and continue walking. I was the only person who was able to bring in my bundle and the bread to the Wysokie bloc. That evening, the Germans ordered all those who had carried bundles of twigs to report for whipping. We cast lots to decide who would report. It fell to Shalom Blumenkrants, Fayvl–Moshe's grandson. He accepted his fate, and reported for the "whipping ceremony." When he returned to the bloc, we rewarded him with a larger slice of bread.

On January 15, 1943, the Germans started to liquidate the Zambrów camp. They announced that people were being sent to work. Hospitalized people were collected and taken to the Christian cemetery, where they were murdered. This took place on a freezing cold night. The sick were flung onto the wagons like pieces of firewood. They were wrapped in rags, half–naked, and exhausted. Some died right there, before any shots were fired.

[Page 203]

The others, who could still stand, were taken out at night in groups, bloc by bloc, and transported by sledge to the Czyżew railway station. Loading onto the sledge was brutal: people were forced to run under a hail of stones, and many died of cold before they reached the station.

In Czyżew, Efrayim Mazur and Leyzer Yellin managed to sneak away and flee, saving themselves. They are living in America today.

When we reached Czyszew, each of us received a slice of bread; we were then shoved into horse–cars, 120 people per car. We thought we were headed for Treblinka, but were "mistaken." Our destination was actually Auschwitz. Several of our townspeople broke the car open, and jumped while the train was rolling. Tragically, only one survived. Peysekh Dolongevitsh hanged himself in Segal's flour mill, and the others were killed by Poles. Only Itsik Volmer was able to find refuge in the house of a Polish woman, whose husband had previously worked in Segal's mill.

We arrived in Auschwitz on January 17, 1943. As in every death camp, the elderly, the women, and the children were immediately separated from the young men and sent directly to the gas chambers. Men capable of work were sent to barracks in the camp. I was one of the latter.

Young women from other towns were generally sent to work as well. However, the women of our town were not so lucky. All, including the young, were sent to their deaths in the gas chambers upon arriving in the infamous camp. The only two girls from Wysokie who remained alive were the Golobradka sisters, because they had been brought from the Pruzhany ghetto. Only four men from Wysokie survived Auschwitz: Moshe Brener, Avraham–Berl Sokol, Leyzer Gaskevitsh, and I.

I spent two years in Auschwitz. In January 1945, I was taken to Mauthausen, and liberated by the U.S. Army on May 7, 1945.

After liberation, I returned to Wysokie. The town was *Judenrein*. Everything was destroyed. I found the brothers Khayim and Peysekh Segal, and about thirty other Jews –the remnant of the Jewish community of Wysokie.

In 1946, I left Poland as a kibbutz member, thanks to the *Brikha* operation, reached Czechoslovakia and continued to Austria and Italy.[5] The British Mandate authorities deported me from the shore of Palestine to Cyprus. I finally reaching the Land of Israel in November, 1947, immediately joined the *Haganah*, and fought in Galilee during Israel's War of Independence. I am now a member of Kibbutz Giv'at Ha–Shlosha.

Translator's Notes:

1. Psalms 129, 3.
2. Bialystok is 55 km from Wysokie.
3. Following the German and Soviet invasion in 1939, most of the ethnically Polish territory came under German control, while the USSR annexed an area with an ethnically diverse population.
4. The *Gendarmerie* was a type of military police.
5. *Brikha* was the underground organization that helped Jewish survivors escape postwar Europe and reach British Mandate Palestine. It ended when Israel declared independence in 1948 and annulled the British "White Paper" that had limited Jewish immigration to Palestine.

[Page 218]

The Cry "Mommy, Daddy" Still Rings in my Ears

Pesach Segal (may his memory be for a blessing), Ramatayim

Translated by Yael Chaver

Before November 1, 1942, we learned that the Germans had ordered 300 wagons, to transport "seedlings" for forest planting. By then, we knew very well what the Germans meant by such "plantings."

No one in the ghetto slept on the night of November 1. A dark terror engulfed us all. We knew that we were doomed to annihilation. Jewish scouts stood at the barbed–wire fences, trying to hear the slightest sound coming from the other side of the ghetto. Suddenly, the rumor spread that the ghetto was surrounded. The night was dark and rainy. Many people crept through the barbed wire strands and sought refuge in the fields and the forests. About 40% of the ghetto's Jews left that night. I was one of them. By morning, I had found my father, and other Jews, in the Masurian forest. By November 14, I had managed to collect my entire family, except for my brother Khayim.

The individual Jews in the forest formed groups. I witnessed heartbreaking scenes. Children were looking for their parents; parents were looking for their children. The cries and screams split the heavens. The childish wail of "Mommy! Daddy!" rings in my ear to this day.

My friend David Guzovsky and I collected a bit of money, walked to the nearby village, where we bought bread. We were able to give slices to twenty children who were wandering in the forest.

The forest crawled with Poles from the vicinity, as well as Russian prisoners of war who had escaped from German camps.

[Page 219]

They abused the Jews and robbed them. In spite of the risk that they would be discovered by the Germans, the Jews clustered in a large group against the robbers.

The days passed and the winter grew fiercer. It snowed, and we were constantly shivering. We dug trenches, camouflaged them, and found temporary refuge. My family and I were in the same refuge as the Hertz and Tenenbaum families.

On Saturday, November 14, we heard shots close by. The moment I raised my head, I realized that I was surrounded by German gendarmes and Polish police. "Raus!" came the order, indicating that we should come out. When I climbed out of the trench, I saw many dead bodies nearby. The young people were ordered into rows of 30. There were several groups of Jews, separate from each other. The chief murderer of the *Gendarmerie* approached us, holding an automatic rifle. His name was Erich, and the Jews called him "Makler" (murderer).[1] When he was five meters away, he ordered, "Bring a member of the Herts family; otherwise, I will shoot 20 Jews." He started shooting without waiting for an answer. My friends David Guzovsky, Biedak, Aharon (Artshe) Herts, David Beker, Hersh–Yitskhak Trestonovitsch, and about 30 other Jews from other groups were shot right there. This terrifying spectacle convinced me that he was planning to kill us all. I didn't panic, but immediately fled into the thick forest. (I later learned that the murderer had turned to my father, Fishl Segal, asking, "Where did you hide your money?" Without waiting for an answer, he shot him on the spot. My mother, Sarah Segal, was slightly wounded.)

When I began to run away, the murderer aimed his rifle at me and opened fire. The bullets flew all around me, breaking off nearby branches. I was not hit, perhaps because I was a well–trained soldier and stayed close to the tree trunks to avoid the bullets.

Those Jews who remained alive, about 100 in all, were returned to Wysokie and jailed. The next day, they were taken to Zambrów, where all the Jews of Łomża were sent.

I was alone in the forest. My mother, my brother Yehoshua, and my sister Rivka were among those returned to Wysokie.

I roamed the forest alone for two days, and then returned to Wysokie, to my home, which was outside the ghetto. I found my brother Khayim, who had hidden with a Polish acquaintance, Danek Kirszenowski.

Wacek Bialicki, the mechanic who worked at our flour mill, helped me find my brother. Bialicki had helped us to build a hideaway in the mill, where we had stayed until December 24, 1942. He had secretly supplied us with food, always fearing his wife or children might find out and turn us over to the Germans.

We were nearly caught one time. The peasant who took over my apartment when we moved into the ghetto informed on us.

On December 24, we had to leave our refuge and find another hiding place. The previous day, December 23, the German *Gendarmerie* came to the home of our host, beat Bialicki severely, and demanded that he turn over the Jews that he was concealing. The Pole claimed that he was not hiding any Jews, and that he had no idea why they were harassing him. The German broke up the floors, knocked on the walls, and dug into the ground in search of the hideout. Luckily for us, and for our savior, they did not discover the refuge. However, after this event we knew that we had to leave; staying any longer would endanger Bialicki's life as well as our own. We had no doubt that the thorough search had been triggered by an informer, and that they would continue to harass the idealistic Pole until we were found.

[Page 220]

We began a new phase of constant wandering and hiding, creeping into barns and granaries, constantly cold and hungry, and afraid of being discovered by Germans or Poles. Besides, we couldn't stay hidden for long and expect miracles. We had to go into the forest from time to time, to seek food. I knew almost all the peasants in the area; before the war, they would come to grind their grain in our mill. They, too, knew me, but few were willing to help us. Some feared the Germans, and others were Jew-haters. Occasionally, we obtained small quantities of food with great difficulty, rarely enough to still our hunger pangs. This was our life until March, 1943.

We invented various tricks in our fight against starvation. One was to knock on a peasant's door and ask to buy schnapps. We knew the peasant custom: if schnapps were set out, they would offer food. This trick worked several times.

One bitterly cold evening, when we were gnawed by hunger, we decided to come out and find some bread at all costs, risking our lives. In the darkness, we slowly moved through the fields toward two tiny flickering lights. Finally, we reached the two shacks with the lights. We knocked at the door and asked for a cigarette light. The Pole, whose name was Marcel Grabowski, invited us in. The inhabitants seemed to be decent people. We then asked to buy a bottle of schnapps. The peasant sent his son to the nearby village of Brika to buy some. My brother stayed inside, while I stepped out to stand guard in case the peasant's son brought the police instead of schnapps. Shortly afterward, the youngster returned and placed a bottle of schnapps on the table. We opened the bottle, saying, "Now, dear hosts, we will drink to your health." I filled two glasses of schnapps, and the peasant set out food. We ate and drank, thanked the peasant for his kindness, and left to continue drifting. Two weeks later, we paid the peasant another visit. This time, we told him that we had hidden a treasure somewhere, and would use it to handsomely reward anyone who concealed us. We agreed on a price. We later learned that we were not the only ones to find refuge with that peasant. He also hid Leyzer Levin and his daughter Pesya in the straw inside the granary. We suggested that he build a hideout according to plans we had drawn up. The entrance was through the cow barn, and the hideout itself was in the field, near the granary, overgrown with tobacco plants.

[Page 221]

We entered this hideout at the end of March, 1943. The peasant, his wife, and his son supplied us with food: a bit of coffee with milk, soup, and bread. We promised him that the war would end in three months–he refused to hide us otherwise. So, when the war did not end as we had promised, they forced us to leave, fearing they would be discovered by the Germans and killed. Several peasants in the area who had concealed Jews were in fact executed by the Germans.

We had no choice but to leave the hideout, and take cover in the grain fields for a while. When news started to come from the front that the Germans were being defeated and the Russians were moving forward, Grabowski allowed us to return to the hideout. We stayed there until Liberation, in August 1944.

Translator's Note:

1. This comment is odd; the Yiddish *makler* means "broker."

———

[Page 225]

Like Thunder on a Clear Day

Avraham Hirshfeld

Translated by Yael Chaver

On September 1, 1939, the first day of the German attack on Poland, the young Jews of our town spontaneously left for other towns or nearby villages.

My brother Barukh (may his memory be for a blessing) and I also fled to the nearby town of Briansk. We saw victims of the bombings there, and the city was very tense. That evening, we decided to return to Wysokie by wagon, sad and dejected. After travelling all night we reached Wysokie in the early morning. The town was unrecognizable. There was a deathly silence, like the silence before a storm. And indeed, our fears were realized. A few minutes later, we started hearing shots. In the center of town, several brave young Poles took up arms and tried to stop the German army at the town gates. The response to this desperate effort was a powerful offensive, including heavy air and ground bombardment. The cannons fired ceaselessly, and aircraft bombed each house in turn, with German precision. Everything was engulfed in fire, and plumes of smoke filled the sky. Everything was burning: the sky above, and the ground underneath. The fire rapidly spread through the town, and people – men, women, and children–rushed out of all the houses. In keeping with Jewish custom, the sick were not abandoned, even under these dire conditions. They were moved out of the houses with their beds, in order to save their lives. The groans and cries of the residents were inaudible in the tumult, as the bombed and shelled town was consumed by flames.

[Page 226]

Along with my mother and my brother Barukh (may God avenge his blood), we found temporary refuge in the house of our friend, the intellectual Yitzkhak Vatnik, whose house had not yet caught fire. My brother Barukh helped the Vatniks to pack their valuables. But our safety was short–lived. We could see the fire approaching. Shots rang through the dense air, the smoke was stifling, and we had trouble breathing. Roofs were lifting, breaking up under the immense pressure, and flying through the air with an unearthly noise.

That first day of the war, with no place to run to, I really understood the meaning of the biblical verse "The sword shall destroy outside; there shall be terror within."[1] We ran instinctively, along with everyone else. But where to? Wherever our legs would take us. We are borne along on the human current to the center of town, running between burning, disintegrating houses. Suddenly, as we reached the fields, our mother collapsed. I protected her with my body from the flying bullets. Gathering up her last strength, she continued running with us. We finally arrived at the Segal–Mayzner flour mill, exhausted.

Night fell. The city is still burning; the flames illuminate the night and intensify our depression and despair.

We form a large black mass of people; we've all lost everything in the blink of an eye. We long for the end of this demonic dance.

Suddenly, I hear the din of approaching tanks, and face the first Nazi soldier. I see him through a fog, as though in a nightmare. His finger is on the trigger, aiming at me. He yells, "*Hände hoch!*" ("Hands up!") I hear his voice and can't understand what he wants. My mother and brother shout to me, "Raise your hands!" I raised my hands, and escaped death.

Despondent and weary, surrounded by German soldiers all night, daylight finally came. Only now can we see the town and its awful destruction. Smoke rises from the skeletons of the incinerated houses, from bent telegraph and streetlight poles, from trees that were warped and distorted by the fire. Only a few scattered houses remain, untouched by the consuming fire. Among them are Segal's grain mill and home, as well as the house on the corner opposite the *Tarbut* school, and the Polish church. We did not know where most of the townspeople had gone.

My mother, brother, and I, found shelter in the house opposite the school, along with many others.

[Page 227]

Some time later, the Germans started shooting at the house's windows. Then the order came for all adult male Jews to report to a certain place. The Germans searched everywhere and dragged out those who did not report. I hid, but they found me and hauled me to the same place. Our numbers kept increasing. Surrounded by soldiers, like a large dark mass, people who are mourning, despairing, and facing death, are walking. Where are they being taken? And why? We are led to the Christian church, not far from the municipal offices. We are stood single–file in long lines, facing machine guns.

The hunt lasted all day. Groups of Poles were also brought in. My brother, who sat nearby, whispered, "If there are Poles here as well, we might be left alive." In the evening of that difficult, fearsome day, we are taken into the church. We lie crowded in a mass on the floor, like marinated herrings, on top of each other. It grows dark. A weak lamp sends a few rays of light through the immense darkness. A German soldier walks among the people lying on the floor, terrifying us.

We got up at dawn, and drank a bit of water in turn, from the same cup. A German soldier stands at the church door, and we file before him as if it were the day of the final judgment.[2] He makes the final decision as to who leaves and who stays. Some old, sick people were allowed to leave. Suddenly my brother Barukh is beside me, ordering me: "Run, flee for your life, you might be able to make it." I ask him, "How about you?" "I'll be fine, don't worry," he replies. In an instant, I manage to evade the German's gaze, and go out.

The solitude outside is terrible: nothing but ruins and wasteland. Luckily, there are no Nazis in the empty street. I run quickly, mustering up the last of my energy, to the house where my mother had been. In a faint, I fall into her arms. She summons up her courage and energy, and finds a Polish wagon–driver. They strike a bargain for him to take me to our relatives in the nearby town of Zambrów. There is no one outside. Alone, I part from my nearest and dearest, lying in the wagon as it rolls along; I'm concealed by clothes and various objects. I finally reached my relatives, the Litavskis.

I reached their house completely exhausted. They were all terrified by the German soldiers, who beat on their doors at night and generally run wild.

My mother's fears for me made her come to Zambrów; a few days later, my brother also arrived. He had fled from the Polish church in Łódź, where the Jews from our town had been marched. He recounted how he and some others had wrenched out a grate in the back wall of the church, then jumped six meters to the street. He told us that the Germans had killed my uncle, Berl Dov Vaynberg, on the way from Zambrów to Łomża.

It was my intention here to describe only the first days after the Nazi invasion of Poland, and the events in Wysokie–Mazowieckie at the time. I am incapable of describing my own experiences afterwards.

Translator's Notes:

1. The quote is from Deuteronomy 32, 25.
2. The phrase *kivney maron* in the Yom Kippur prayer *U–netaneh tokef*, describing souls passing before God, is usually interpreted as sheep awaiting their final fate.

[Page 231]

The "Miracle" in Moscow

Shimon Kahanovitsh (may his memory be for a blessing)

Translated by Yael Chaver

There have been no miracles in Russia since the Russian revolution, although Moscow was home to forty times forty churches. However, it was in this city, where there were no miracles, that I experienced a miracle, at a time when miracles did not happen.

But let's tell the whole story as it happened.

When I was four or five years old, my parents traveled from Bialystok to Wysokie-Mazowieckie. This was during World War I, in 1916–1917. As far as I was concerned, Wysokie was the town where I grew up, studied, and joined a Zionist youth group. All my friends and acquaintances were from this town.

My connections with Wysokie continued even after when we moved back to Bialystok in 1931, as we owned flour mills there and shipped flour from Wysokie to Bialystok. The town was very dear to me.

World War II broke out in 1939, and the Bolsheviks took Bialystok, according to the infamous Molotov–Ribbentrop agreement. My situation now became much worse. My parents were considered capitalists, although we all worked hard to make a living. We all underwent various harassments; but the worst was that at any minute we could be exiled to Siberia, under the ongoing project of "deporting disloyal elements."

[Page 232]

I had to do something to save my family. Using my old connections, I was able to obtain "proletarian" documents, proving that I was a car mechanic and driver. This was partly true, as I really was my parent's driver, and I was very familiar with the mechanisms of cars. I also became the formal head of the family, and was thus able to place the entire family under my protection as proletarians. This saved my parents from being exiled to the remote, cold regions of Russia.

As a bona fide proletarian, I began looking for work. My connections helped me find work in the transportation section of a large department store. Naturally, these connections were expensive, and gift–giving was a regular arrangement. But it was a solution.

I had two direct supervisors in the department store, one political and the other commercial. I got the job through connections, as they were not local but rather had come from Russia. I thanked them in various ways for hiring me.

This lasted for some time; we slowly became accustomed to the new situation. However, it was not for long.

On June 22, 1941, Hitler's Germany – Russia's partner in the division of Poland – suddenly began bombing Russian towns, and German armies crossed the borders. Bialystok was heavily bombed as early as that first day. The town was in an uproar, especially among the Russians. We, the locals, were somewhat deluded and believed in the great power of Russia.

2.

My supervisor called me in on that first day, June 22, 1941. He wrote out a travel pass, and told me to fill up gasoline for a trip of several hundreds of kilometers. He had not yet told me where to go. I went back home, said my farewells, and told them I was leaving for only a few days. I had no inkling that I was setting out on a long, distant road...

[Page 233]

The pass was for Minsk. I drove the wife of the political supervisor, as well as the entire family of the commercial director. This director was a Russian Jew named Lyova Paley. En route to Minsk, we saw masses of dead bodies on the roads. The German murderers bombed incessantly. The roads were packed; one could travel only by night.

We arrived in Minsk the next day. There was massive destruction; the city was on fire. No one was in charge. My supervisor Lyova Paley was able to obtain some gasoline, and we quickly left the burning city. We set out for Moscow.

We arrived in Moscow on the third day. I had trouble adjusting to the situation. Only one thing concerned me: the fate of my parents and family. I could think only of returning to Bialystok as soon as possible. My mission was completed, and I could go back home.

I went to the post office to send a telegram, and received the terrible news that Bialystok had been occupied by the Germans, and contact had been severed. I was at a loss, completely paralyzed. Now, when my parents need me so badly, I am completely cut off from them. I did not know what to do.

Lyova Paley invited me to visit him. I felt close to him. He had helped me settle into my job. Actually, I had compensated him considerably, but it was nonetheless a great favor, which I appreciated. We had become good friends during the short period we had worked together.

He took me into a small room, and made up a bed for me on the floor. Exhausted from my trip and my difficult experiences, I fell sound asleep. Loud hammering on the door did not awake me, but I was woken by a boot blow to my side.[1]

Two NKVD agents were standing over me, ordering me to get dressed.[2] I had been sleeping in my clothes. I pulled on my boots, and waited. The agents took me and Paley somewhere. At our destination, my escorts received written confirmation that the "merchandise" had been delivered; they then left.

[Page 234]

We were left alone, each deep in sad thoughts for our own reasons. I did not think about the past or the future. I thought that there had been some mistake, and everything would be cleared up. True, in the course of the Soviet regime in Bialystok, I had already heard about the arbitrary ways of the NKVD; but, like every young person, I did not take it to heart but shoved the knowledge deep down.

Paley, on the other hand, was experienced in Soviet matters, and knew very well why he had fallen into such heavy gloom. He understood our difficult situation. He knew enough not to try and escape; he was also aware of what was in store for him.

I had trouble convincing him to tell me everything and describe our tragic situation. Once I understood it and grasped it fully, I was even more despondent. Paley consoled me, saying that I would get away with a light sentence or nothing at all, because I was not the target. They needed me against him. He, for his part, was threatened with a death sentence.

I started thinking about how to help him. I couldn't permit him to pay with his life. I felt conscience–bound to help him. I considered possibilities for a long time, until I finally came up with the following plan:

I tore up the "pass" and destroyed it. As long as there was nothing in writing – "evidence" – we could attempt to create a different version of the trip could be attempted, one that would not exacerbate matters. I first gave Paley my solemn word that I would not cause him any harm. I told him to keep to the same phrasing, the same version, and on no account to believe the words of the investigators, or that either of us would confess, or that there was "secret evidence."

I then proposed the following plan, that we would both stick to: we had received the "pass" from a high–ranking director named Skorbitsh. Skorbitsh had remained in Bialystok, and no one would be able to check whether he had or had not given us the pass, as Bialystok was busy with other matters. As there had been no official announcement, and no one knew of the incident, we could demand that inquiries be made as to whether it was true. As far as the "pass" was concerned, I took it upon myself to manipulate it. In short, our version was that Skorbitsh had given us the "pass" and sent us off. In this way, I was hoping to thank Paley for the favor he once did me.

[Page 235]

3

The next morning, we were separated. I was called to the investigator's office, and asked at first about incidental matters, such as how I found life under the Soviet authorities. As usual, I said that it was only thanks to the Soviet authorities that I had steady work and good earnings, unlike earlier in Poland. At that point he asked what seemed to be the main question: who had issued the ticket. I pretended to search for it, and said that I assumed it was in the car. As there had been checkpoints every few kilometers, I had preferred to leave it in the car. He then asked who had given it to me. I said that Skorbitsh had called me in, given me the "pass," then summoned Paley, and ordered us to go. Now the investigator posed the most important question: why did such a high–ranking official as Skorbitsh give me the document, when ordinarily – as I had said in earlier statements – the "passes" would be written out by the garage manager. I had an explanation ready: it had been Sunday, and not everyone was at work. I also asked him to ask Skorbitsh in Bialystok.

The interrogator asked me what we had done in Minsk. I said that it had been none of my business and that I was responsible only for driving.

I was taken back to jail, but not for long. They soon summoned me to another questioning, even more severe. I stuck to my version. The interrogator claimed that he had not found the "pass" in the car, and that Skorbitsh had refuted my explanations.

I told the same story at the third interrogation as well. The interrogator threatened me, and tried persuasion as well. "What harm would it do for you to sign a statement that Paley is guilty?" All this was of no avail. I repeated my explanations.

I did not see Paley, but I hoped that he, too, was staying with the story. Up to this point, the arrest had not been difficult. Now, it worsened. I was immediately summoned to another interrogation, again warned to tell the truth, or I would stand trial.

[Page 236]

Indeed, the trial soon took place. I saw Paley there. There was a single judge. He brushed away my explanations. and announced that Paley was the one who had written out the "pass." Once again, I repeated the explanations I had given in the interrogations. Paley also offered the same explanations.

The trial broke for five minutes, and resumed with the following sentence.

Paley received twenty years for escaping, and I received fifteen years.

We were again separated, and this time taken to prison. My heart was heavy. Fifteen years is no small thing; who knew whether I would ever see my family again. But my conscience was clear. I had done everything it dictated. I did achieve something: the judge hadn't been certain, and hadn't given a death sentence.

4

Late that night in the prison, a Russian official appeared; as was customary, asked whether anyone wished to complain of anything. The Russians knew enough not to complain. It was totally pointless, and might lead to serious trouble. They always answered, "No complaints." But I was a "greenhorn," and announced that I wanted to complain. The official asked whether I had been mistreated by anyone in the administration or the cell. I explained that I had no complaints about them, but that it was a matter better discussed in private. He was curious, and told me to come with him.

He heard me out. At first, he was hostile, because I did not accept the court's legality; but when he heard me out he changed his mind. I demanded that he set up a phone call for me with Skorbitsh, to prove my claims. Apparently, this convinced him to promise me that he would help me to make an appeal. He also told that I would be able to reduce my sentence by five years. However, it would be far better for me if I put the entire blame on Paley, in which case I would go completely free. "Ten years is a lot," he argued, "for such a young person."

[Page 237]

I categorically rejected the idea that I should inform on Paley. My firmness apparently convinced him. He promised to help.

The trial resumed. Both Paley and I repeated every detail that we had provided in the previous trial and during the interrogations. It seemed that our explanations, which matched, were logical as well. So – mainly because they could not contact Skorbitsh – everything worked in our favor and the great "miracle" occurred: we were both set completely free. I found it hard to believe, although I had hoped and planned for this outcome the entire time. Paley was even more surprised and astounded. As a Russian, he knew that such things did not happen in Russia.

I felt a mixture of joy and sadness. Joy at being freed, and sadness at the news that the Germans were advancing and the Soviet army was retreating from city after city in an "orderly fashion." I was living proof of this "orderliness."

Paley wanted to take me with him to Tashkent, where he had family and a place to live. It was indeed a very good plan, but I was reluctant to go far away from my home. Meanwhile, I had heard over the radio that men born in 1912 were being drafted into army service. I was afraid to go anywhere, as I might pay dearly. I was already under suspicion, and could easily have been tried for desertion.

We parted with heavy hearts. He gave me fifty rubles, as he himself was short of money. He also advised me to go to the management of the department store, where I received 50 more rubles. I asked them to connect me with the army's recruiting office, as I wanted to join the army. They sent me to the military commissariat; their connections helped me to get a job in a garage, where drivers were recruited. The fighting forces would regularly take men out and send them to different battalions.

I worked in the garage for a longer time. Conditions were very harsh; there was no place to sleep, as it was a temporary location. I grew tired of being homeless, and asked the garage manager to be posted to a battalion. He was very friendly. He recommended me to his acquaintance, Major Lyapushkin, who commanded an administrative company. He also gave me a good vehicle; this was crucial, as it enabled a driver could fulfil his orders as well as possible, and thereby gain a reputation as a useful and vital person.

[Page 238]

Major Lyapushkin was a fine person. He transferred me to a battalion that was stationed in Moscow. As I was a good mechanic, I quickly became highly appreciated by the unit.

Time went on, and winter came. Conditions at the front worsened. There was heavy fighting in Vyazma.[3] The front came ever nearer to Moscow, and the city was hastily evacuated. The government and all its offices were transferred to Kuibyshev. I was very busy with this project. I moved archives and documents from the Kremlin to Kuibyshev. I also transported materials and necessities to the front.

December, 1941, saw severe frost. We were ordered to take felt boots to the nearby front. On one of these trips, there was great tumult at the front, and we were ordered to return. However, I was not able to travel for long, as my vehicle was bombed.

I woke up in a field hospital with cuts on my face from shattered glass. Someone had found me bleeding in the field and brought me to the hospital.

When I regained some strength, I was not sent back to my battalion. New battalions were quickly organized in the confusion. They handed me a rifle and sent me to one such battalion. This was how I became a complete front–line soldier.

Our battalion had no vehicle at its disposal, but did need one urgently. Many broken–down cars lay all around; choosing wisely, it was possible to patch together a car from their parts. There were only two types of engines in Russia at the time. I proposed to my lieutenant that I should be given tools and workers, and I would assemble a working car. He liked the idea, and I carried out the project. Three days later, a car was ready.

I had pieced the car together so that I would have a chance to rejoin my battalion in Moscow. I waited for a while, until I was able to travel to Moscow. Naturally, I had no documents allowing me to enter the capital. Instead, I had some brandy. Thanks to the liquor, I was able to telephone Major Lyapushkin.

[Page 239]

The major was happy to see me, and came to get me in person. He immediately took me back into the battalion, repainted my car, gave it a number, and I was once again "at home."

6.

The Germans began their spring offensive in April 1942. The fighting was fierce, and a regular flow of supplies was necessary. I was near Vyazma several times. Once, I was there during a German advance; before we knew it, we – a group of drivers with cars–were encircled by the Germans.

The first thing I needed to do was to separate myself from my fellow drivers; I was afraid they might say that I was a Jew. As the Germans took very many prisoners, I was able to join a different group. Escaping was impossible, and there was nowhere to hide, either. Having no choice, I was shoved into a barracks with my new friends.

The Germans did not know how to drive cars under the conditions of a Russian winter. Thus, I had no trouble working as a driver once again. But being a driver under German command was not easy. They were very nervous, and suspicious that anyone might be a Jew or a partisan. They tried to find out several times whether I was Jewish. On one occasion, two high–ranking Gestapo officers asked me in German whether I was hungry, and ordered me to eat.[4] I pretended not to understand, although I was very hungry. Incidentally, they both spoke fluent Russian.

I was terribly afraid of a mishap. How long could this last? The Germans acted wildly, shooting people for the slightest reason. Obviously, the situation increased their edginess. They were also in a panic because of the partisans; this was clear from their expressions. They would go on rampages and shoot entire groups of men. The slightest suspicion or remark would lead to the shooting of anyone they considered a potential enemy. My situation became less bearable by the day. I felt that it could not last long. I was resigned to anything.

Deep inside, I had faith that I would be rid of them and not have to see their savage faces. I could not stop thinking about escaping. The idea obsessed me; one day I took my vehicle, made sure I had an iron bar – one could not steal a weapon – and set out with a ration of bread. I managed to get far away from the unit's position.

[Page 240]

I crashed the car in a ditch, and went into the forest – there were many of those in the region. I was hoping to penetrate the front lines and rejoin my battalion. Going through German–occupied territory was out of the question, both because of the Germans and the hostile attitude of the local population.

I lay hidden in the forest all day, afraid I would be noticed. It grew very cold at night, but my only option was to wait. I did not know which way to go.

I lay there in the murky darkness a long time. At one point I heard steps. People were walking, and moreover – speaking Russian. I could not make out what they were saying, as they were too far away. I was careful not to reveal myself, as I was afraid and did not know who they were. They went up to a pit, and either put something in or took something out. I decided that the first thing was to find out what was in the pit. So I waited for them to leave.

They did leave soon afterward. I waited for some light, and came up to the pit. Once I had removed the camouflage, I discovered an arms cache. I selected a revolver and took a large amount of ammunition. An armed man had to be reckoned with, regardless of the situation.

Now armed, I still did not know what to do next or where to go. Having no better choice, I lay in the forest for another day, waiting for the nocturnal visitors. In the meantime, I concealed myself with branches so as not to be discovered accidentally. I waited for the pitch–black night.

The same people came back late that night. I quietly sneaked behind them, holding my weapon, and asked them in Russian who they were.

After a brief conversation, we came to an understanding. I told them my story, and they said that they were a small partisan group, which blew up railway lines that carried German troop trains.

[Page 241]

They supplied their own food, requisitioning it from the peasants at night. There was a Jew among them, with whom I became friendly.

I had a bad feeling about the place. I very much wanted to return to my battalion. Finally, I convinced my commander that I had received permission, as well as help, to return to my unit.

The way back, regardless of whatever help I received, was very difficult and fraught with danger. That is another story, and I don't want to describe that time here.

7.

I finally returned to my battalion –my second home – uninjured and in good condition. Once again, I sat at the wheel and transported vehicles to the front lines. The further away the line moved from the capital, the longer were my trips. I gradually moved westward, along with the front. This continued until 1944.

The Soviet army then entered former Polish territory. Familiar names of cities and towns began to appear in the communiques. I had mixed feelings. On the one hand, we knew about the terrible annihilation, yet on the other hand we hoped for...maybe...something.

Finally, I heard the names of Bialystok and Wysokie in the communiques. I was anxious to leave. When they dispatched a column of 150 trucks to Ostrów Mazowiecka, I was, naturally, one of the first to go.[5]

Near Vawkavysk, I first became aware of the great disaster. My aim was to see Wysokie and Bialystok – two places where I hoped to meet someone of my kin. I feared the encounter with reality, but had to go. After all, miracles can still happen.

I requested my commander for permission to visit my two home towns on the trip. He gave me permission to make a detour and see – even though briefly – my home towns.

Our house in Bialystok was occupied by strange Poles. The curtains, couch, tablecloths, and other objects were ours. They were familiar, beloved, and comforting. But the people in the house made them seem alien. The Poles were alarmed when they first saw me. Besides, I was wearing a Russian uniform. However, when they realized that I was paying no attention to the plundered property and was interested only in my kin, they calmed down.

[Page 242]

That night, I slept in Bialystok, if insomnia and being overcome by profound sorrow count as sleeping.

I entered Wysokie early the next morning.

The formerly Jewish town was now *Judenrein.*[6] There was not a single Jew to be seen. The street was full of unfamiliar, hostile faces. I met a Polish acquaintance named Podszilo, who told me that my entire family had been killed and that nearly all the Jews had been murdered. The few surviving Jews were living in Peysekh Segal's mill. Among them was Pianko. I hurried over there, but could not stay long, as I had to catch up with my column.

I returned as soon as I had reported in Ostrów Mazowiecka. Back in Wysokie, I wanted to meet my surviving friends. We shared our troubles. They coaxed me to leave military service, wear civilian clothing, and join them.

I dearly wanted to be among Jews, especially as these were my own people. Yet I did not want to be a deserter. It was not in my nature to hide. My military service was relatively comfortable, and the main thing was that I wasn't being sent to the front lines. Besides, my work as a driver provided me with better conditions than most.

True, there was no shortage of unpleasantness and anti–Semitism here, either. Once, I was even slightly punished. The incident was as follows:

My vehicle was excellent. Yet once I couldn't start the engine. I tried everything, checked all the parts again, cleaned and polished the engine, but it didn't start. Then one of my helpers told me that someone must have poured sugar into the gas tank, preventing the engine from igniting.

I was very annoyed by this, and decided to teach the anti–Semite a lesson, or even worse things would happen. I informed my superior that I would not sleep in the barracks as I needed to go somewhere. He gave me permission, smiling ambiguously. Itook an iron bar, crawled into my vehicle, and lay down to wait for the hooligan. He showed up late at night, first inspecting his own vehicle and then approaching mine.

[Page 243]

He took out a packet of sugar, unscrewed the top of the gas tank, and started pouring in the sugar. At that instant he was attacked by me. I beat him up. People came running when they heard his screams.

We were both arrested. Proof of his guilt and the damage he had caused was clear: the sugar was strewn on the floor. He received a harsh sentence: to be sent to the front. I was also punished, for fighting–to chop wood for two weeks, and do no driving during that time.

I recount this in order to show that the battalion was none too nice to me. If I had committed one more crime, I would have been sent to the front. In order to be a good driver, one had to commit crimes, wheel and deal, skim off the top, take one's cut. In such situations, the slightest mistake could lead to a sentence of being sent to the front to join a labor battalion.

I decided to stay within the law. I remained in the service. I served in Moscow until May 1945, the end of the war. I shuttled back and forth to the front, driving vehicles and waiting for the end of my service.

Finally, I lived to see it. The war ended. Moscow celebrated the victory. But in my heart there was only a deep wound. It was December 1945 before I was demobilized. As a "defender" of Moscow, I had the right to become a resident of the city – a privilege that any Russian citizen would have counted himself lucky to have.

However, I only thanked them for the privilege, and left for Poland. At first I went to Bialystok, and realized that I couldn't stay there – the tragedy was too profound. I then went to Wrocław. However, I could not be at peace in this Lower Silesian city, where remnants of survivors and repatriates from Russia had gathered. I stayed for a few weeks, long enough to work a bit, purchase new clothes, and appear more presentable.

It was a period of chaos. No one knew what the next day would bring. I crossed the border to Czechoslovakia and entered a displaced person camp. As a driver, I placed myself at the disposal of the *Brikha* – the Jewish operation that smuggled Jews into the Land of Israel.[7] Enormous streams of Jews were smuggled out of the camps to locations closer to the borders of the Land of Israel, and eventually transported there on ships. The British ruthlessly persecuted both the young people who carried out the operation and the fleeing Jews.

My next stop was Kassel–Frankfurt.[8] I had been doing this work since my youth, and continued doing it out of a deep love for Zion, combined with the bitter experiences of recent years. The entire operation was linked with the years of misery that people had endured. Once again, I had no permanent location. For a time, I worked as a driver for an American organization. Fate did not want me to give up the wheel.

I was tired of moving around, and sought a place where I could rest my head. The prospects of traveling to the Land of Israel were poor, and I had no patience for waiting. I was on my own, with no one to advise me.

At that time, various consulates were registering potential immigrants. People found relatives all over the world, requested documents, and registered wherever possible. I did the same.

The U.S. consul was the first to call me. It was in this way that I came to America in 1948.

(This chapter was written by Mr. Kirsh, who interviewed S. Kahanovitsh [may his memory be for a blessing])

Translator's Notes:

1. The Yiddish clause states, "I was awakened by a head (*kop*) to my side." I believe this is a typo for *klap* (blow); and have translated it accordingly.
2. The NKVD was the Soviet secret police
3. In late 1941, Vyazma (on the outskirts of Moscow) was one of the key points in the battle for the Soviet capital against the German army. The German advance was halted in January 1942.
4. The Yiddish term here, *geshapo*, is obviously a typo.
5. Ostrów Mazowiecka and Wysokie Mazowieckie are neighboring counties.
6. The writer uses the Nazi German term for "cleansed of Jews."
7. *Brikha* was the clandestine organized effort that helped Jewish survivors escape Post–World War II Europe to British Mandate Palestine, in violation of the British White Paper of 1939.
8. I was not able to determine this reference.

———

[Page 245]

My Town, Wysokie–Mazowieckie

Motl Ptashevitsh, New York

Translated by Yael Chaver

Among fields and forests,
With villages all around,
Lies my town, Wysokie–Mazowiecki
My home town.

Streets and alleys,
Non–Jews all around,
A large market square
with room for thousands.

A large County building,
Stalls and shops at the sides,
Two pumps to fight fires,
And tools for firefighters.

Not one to lag behind,
My town is as good as the others –
It too built a prison
On the river bank.

Houses built of wood
And some brick walls – not too many
This was my town,
Which led a quiet life.

A community hospital, a travelers'
A cemetery, near a
Poorhouse for the
Wandering indigents.

A rabbi, so imposing,
There's none like him any more!
We were the envy of
The neighboring towns.

[Page 246]

Gardens, orchards,
Roads for pleasure walks,
For young peoples' fun,
And political debates.

Proud young folks,
Such joy in life,
Defending honor,
Striving for better times.

They started political parties,
Clubs for sports and drama,
For bodily strength
And intellectual improvement.

Fine homeowners,
Good working Jews,
Each lived within his means
In happiness.

They included
Shopkeepers, craftsmen
Of all types,
As well as great merchants.

Neighbors were like brothers,
Held each other's hands
To offer help,
As much as possible.

The insane,
The physically damaged,
Were also there.
Could a town be otherwise?

[Page 247]

This is how I see my town,
If I remember correctly.
That's where my cradle stood,
The scene of my childhood.

An archenemy[1] came,
May his name and memory be blotted

He turned my town into a ruin.
What a horror— woe is us!

O, Wysokie, my lovely town,
I feel the disaster that struck you,
And I say: I'll never forget
As long as my eyes are open.

And to you, my brothers,
Whose lives were cut so short,
Instead of saying *Kaddish*[2]
I will say different words.

Let the words
I write with such anguish
Be a perpetual candle for your souls,
An eternal monument.

Translator's Notes:

1. The author uses the biblical term *Amalek*, which conventionally denotes traditional enemies of the Jews.
2. *Kaddish* is the traditional mourner's prayer.

————

[Page 248]

Pictures

Translated by Yael Chaver

**Plaque commemorating Wysokie-Mazowieckie in the Chamber of the Holocaust,
Mount Zion, Jerusalem**

Wysokie survivors at the monument in the Forest of the Martyrs

[Page 249]

The audience at the annual memorial service for the martyrs of Wysokie, on the 11th day of Shevat

The audience at the annual memorial service for the martyrs of Wysokie, on the 11th day of Shevat

[Pages 251 - 256]

The Martyrs List of the Holy Communities
of Wysokie Mazowiecki and Jablonka

May God Revenge Their Blood

Wysokie Mazowiecki

Note From the Project
Coordinator:

The names of many of the murdered Jews listed in this Yizkor Book are also included in the Yad Vashem Central Database of Shoah Victims. In addition, Pages of Testimony for other victims from Visoka-Mozovietsk have also been submitted by family members and friends. These Pages of Testimony in many instances provide names of parents, spouses, children, occupations, and ages of the victims. The database can be searched by an individual's name or by town name. (Please note that the database uses a number of different spellings for the name of the town.) The Pages of Testimony also list the name of the person providing the information (the Submitter). The database can also be searched by the name of the Submitter, which may lead the researcher to other family members.

א A,E,I,O	ב B	ג G	ד D	ה H	ו V,W	ז Z,S	ח H	ט T	י Y	כ K,C
ל L	מ M	נ N	ס S	ע E	פ ף F,P	צ S,Z	ק K,C	ר R	ש SH,S	ת T,S

Surname	Name
א **Aleph**	
OLSZA	Berl
OLSZA	Sara
OLSZA	Chaim Icchak
OLSZA	Rywka
OLSZA	Pinchas Eli
OLSZA	Rachel
OPTAL	Janina
AMITIN	Ester
OBAGEWICZ	Josef
OBAGEWICZ	Itta
OBAGEWICZ	Abraham
OBAGEWICZ	Szajndel
OSAWJECZKI	Icchak Mordechai
OSAWJECZKI	Liba
OSAWJECZKI	Cipa
OSAWJECZKI	Mosze Meir
OSAWJECZKI	Dawid Lajbel
OSAWJECZKI	Miriam
OSAWJECZKI	Chaim
OSAWJECZKI	Lajbel
OSAWJECZKI	Raczka

OSAWJECZKI	Lajbel
OSAWJECZKI	Mala
OSAWJECZKI	children
AGOREK	Mosze
AGOREK	Cypa
AGOREK	Jakob
AGOREK	Szajndel
AGOREK	Arie
AGOREK	Liba
AGOREK	Mosze
AGOREK	Zalman
AGOREK	Ester
AGOREK	Ajzik
AGOREK	Alta
AGOREK	Elka
AGOREK	Bendet
AGOREK	Chana
AGOREK	Henia Fajga
AGOREK	Dawid
AGOREK	Jenta
AGOREK	Chaia Sara
AGOREK	Dwora
AGOREK	Chinka
AGOREK	Meir
ADASZKA	Israel
ADASZKA	Lajbel
ADASZKA	Lea
ADASZKA	Ettl

בּ

Bet

BURSZTEIN	Henia Rachel
BURSZTEIN	Eliezer
BURSZTEIN	Kalman
BURSZTEIN	Fruma
BURSZTEIN	Toyba
BURSZTEIN	Etka
BURSZTEIN	Mendel
BURSZTEIN	Ester
BURSZTEIN	Menachem
BURSZTEIN	Rachel
BURSZTEIN	Dan
BURSZTEIN	Michael
BURSZTEIN	Alta
BURSZTEIN	Chaja Sara
BURSZTEIN	Jakob
BURSZTEIN	Rywka
BIALYSOCZKI	Lajbel
BERMAN	Abraham
BERMAN	Liba
BERMAN	Chawa
BERMAN	Toiba
BERMAN	Jakob
BERMAN	Lea
BERMAN	Sara
BERMAN	Rachel
BOJMAN	Eliezer Yehuda
BOJMAN	Hadassa
BUWLOWICZ	Zelig

BUWLOWICZ	Liba
BUWLOWICZ	Abraham
BRENER	The children
BRENER	Gdalyahu
BRENER	Zelda
BRENER	Chancze
BRENER	Nachke
BRENER	Israel
BRENER	The son
BUCHENHOLC	Mosze
BUCHENHOLC	Chemda
BERNHOLC	
BRIZMAN	Toiba
BROIDE	Hillel
BROIDE	Dina
BROIDE	Eliezer
BERGER	Abrham Ajzik
BRODERZON	Sara
BRODERZON	Szymon
BRODERZON	Bluma Lea
BRZEZE	Welwel
BRZEZE	Ester
BIELSKI	Motel
BIELSKI	Mosze
BIELSKI	Minia
BURAK	Elka
BRIKER	Sachka
BRIKER	The wife
BRIKER	The children

BRIKER	Szlomo
BUKINSKI	
BLUMSZTEJN	Szmuel Nachman
BLUMSZTEJN	Fradel
BLUMSZTEJN	Chana Ester
BLUMSZTEJN	Lea
BLUMSZTEJN	Icchak Lajb
BLUMSZTEJN	Lajbke
BIEDAK	Dawid
BIEDAK	The wife
BIEDAK	3 children
BIEDAK	Anszel
BIEDAK	The wife
BIEDAK	4 children
BIEDAK	Josef
BIEDAK	The wife
BIEDAK	2 children
BIEDAK	Chaim
BIEDAK	The wife
BIEDAK	3 children
BALGMAN	Zisa

א

Gimmel

GOLDMAN	Baruch
GOLDMAN	Zisa
GOLDMAN	The children
GOLDMAN	Lajma
GOLDMAN	Alta
GOLDMAN	Sara

GOLDMAN	Abraham
GOLDMAN	Kalman
GOLDMAN	Mosze
GOLDMAN	Fajga
GOLDMAN	The children
GARZSZALCZANE	Ester Dwora
GARZSZALCZANE	Lajb
GARZSZALCZANE	Sara Fajga
GARZSZALCZANE	Liba
GOLDMAN	Chana
GOLDMAN	Fradel
GOLOMBEK	Meir Dawid
GOLOMBEK	Henia Doba
GOLOMBEK	Sara
GOLOMBEK	The children
GOLOMBEK	Chaim Reuwen
GOLOMBEK	Pessach Mordechai
GOLOMBEK	Nachman
GOLOMBEK	Chaia
GRANICA	Markel
GRANICA	Szaszka
GRANICA	Szepsl
GRANICA	Chaia
GOLDA	Mosze
GOLDA	Frajda
GOLDA	Fradel
GOLDA	Mindl
GUZOWSKI	(Dow) Berl
GUZOWSKI	Abraham

GUZOWSKI	Miriam
GAWOWICZ	Sara Bajla
GAWOWICZ	The children
GLISZINSKI	Cwi (Herszel)
GLISZINSKI	Alta
GLISZINSKI	Abraham
GLISZINSKI	Eli
GLISZINSKI	Sara
GLISZINSKI	Jeszayahu
GRINSTEIN	Icchak Dawid
GRINSTEIN	Chinka
GRINSTEIN	Yehudit
GRINSTEIN	Becalel
GRINBERG	Eliahu
GRINBERG	Motel
GRINBERG	Jakob
GRINBERG	Icchak
GRINBERG	Alter
GRINBERG	Chana
GRINBERG	The children
GOLABRADKI	Chanoch (Henoch)
GOLABRADKI	Rachel
GOLABRADKI	Doba
GOLABRADKI	Jerchmiel
GOLABRADKI	Chaia
GOLDIN	Jeszayahu
GOLDIN	Abraham Hersz
GOLDIN	wife of Abraham Hersz
GOLDIN	Dina and her

	husband
ד **Dalet**	
DEUTCHIMINER	Symcha
DEUTCHIMINER	Rachel (Rochka)
DEUTCHIMINER	Chaim
DEUTCHIMINER	Pesach
DOLENGEWICZ	Ettl
DOLENGEWICZ	Motel
DOLENGEWICZ	Bercze
DOLENGEWICZ	Israel
DOLENGEWICZ	Szoszka
DOLENGEWICZ	Mordechai
DOLENGEWICZ	Jakob
DOLENGEWICZ	Icchak
DOLENGEWICZ	Mjeta
DOLENGEWICZ	Fradel
DOLENGEWICZ	Pesach
DOLENGEWICZ	Miriam
ה **Hay**	
HERC	Abraham
HERC	Minia
HERC	Chaim
HERC	Mosze
HERC	Aharon
HERC	The wife
HOZE	Symcha Bonim
HIRSZFELD	Miriam

HIRSZFELD	Baruch

‪ו‬

Vov

WIZENBERG	Icchak
WIZENBERG	Jeszayahu
WINER	Szymon
WINER	Chaia
WINER	Szajna
WINER	Jeszayahu
WANSOWER	Eliahu
WANSOWER	Szprinca
WANSOWER	Benjamin
WOTNIK	Icchak
WOTNIK	Dwora
WOTNIK	Aba
WOTNIK	A son
WOTNIK	A daughter
WAJSOCZEK	Israel
WAJSOCZEK	A wife
WAJSOCZEK	children
WAJSOCZEK	Szymon
WAJSOCZEK	Brajna
WAJSOCZEK	Gutka
WAJSOCZEK	Noach
WAJNKRANC	Jerchmiel
WAJNKRANC	Liba
WAJNKRANC	Aharon
WAJNKRANC	Jakob
WAJNKRANC	Sara

WAJNKRANC	Symcha
WRUBEL	Josef
WRUBEL	Miriam (Rikel)
WRUBEL	Golda
WRUBEL	Pesach
WRUBEL	Dwora
WRUBEL	Mordechai
WRUBEL	A wife
WRUBEL	A daughter
WRUBEL	Meir
WRUBEL	Lea
WRUBEL	2 sons
WRUBEL	Mosze
WRUBEL	The wife
WRUBEL	The children
WRUBEL	Chaia
WRUBEL	Ester (Kolisza)
WRUBEL	Herszel
WRUBEL	Lozer (Eliezer)
WRUBEL	Szoszka (Szoszana)
WRUBEL	Chana
WRUBEL	Jakob (Jankel) wife and 4 children
WRUBEL	Bracha and her 2 children
WRUBEL	Meir
WRUBEL	Abraham
WRUBEL	Sara
WRUBEL	Mordechai

WRUBEL	Chanan
WRUBEL	Icchak
WILEMOWSKI	Fajwel Mosze
WILEMOWSKI	Brajna
WILEMOWSKI	Lajbel
WILEMOWSKI	The wife
WILEMOWSKI	The children
WETER	Abraham Baruch
WAJNBERG	Berl
WAJNBERG	Reuwen
WIROWNIK	
WOFNICKI	Herszel
WOFNICKI	Gutka
WOFNICKI	The children
WOJECHA	Jakob Yehuda Chanoch
WOJECHA	Sara Jache
WOJECHA	Fola
WOJECHA	Szmuel Meir
WOJECHA	Liba
WOJECHA	Lea Rajzel
WOJECHA	Pinchas
WOJECHA	Chaim
WOJECHA	Lea
WOJECHA	Josef
WOJECHA	Sara
WAJSBARD	Szmuel
WAJSBARD	3 children
WAJSBARD	Mosze
WAJSBARD	Musze

WAJSBARD	Szprinca
WAJSBARD	Ester
WAJSBARD	son

ז

Zion

ZWANOWICZ	Mosze
ZWANOWICZ	Szajna
ZWANOWICZ	Doba
ZWANOWICZ	Elia
ZAK	Alter
ZAK	Roszka
ZAK	Symcha Welwel
ZAK	Golda, Dr.
ZAK	Yehuda
ZAKIMOWICZ	Yehuda
ZAKIMOWICZ	Bajlka
ZAKIMOWICZ	Sima, Dr.
ZABLUDOWICZ	Chaia Kajla
ZABLUDOWICZ	Abraham Hersz
ZILBERFENIG	Yehuda
ZILBERFENIG	Libcza
ZILBERFENIG	Perl
ZILBERFENIG	Herszel
ZLOTALAW	Jakob
ZLOTALAW	wife
ZLOTALAW	2 daughters
ZLOTALAW	Meir
ZLOTALAW	Chancza
ZLOTALAW	Issaschar

ZLOTALAW	Beniamin
ZLOTALAW	Szlomo
ZLOTALAW	Tojba
ZLOTALAW	Rachel
ZLOTALAW	Chaia
ZLOTALAW	Malka
ZLOTALAW	Ajzik
ZLOTALAW	Pinchas
ZLOTALAW	Sara
ZLOTALAW	Herszel
ZLOTALAW	Rywka
ZLODKA	Miriam
ZLODKA	Lea and A daughter
ZLODKA	Daniel Josef
ZLODKA	Brajna
ZLODKA	Szalom Icchak
ZLODKA	Tojba
ZLODKA	Cwiya
ZLODKA	Jakob
ZLODKA	Malka
ZLODKA	2 daughters
ZIBICZA	Josef
ZIBICZA	Elka
ZIBICZA	Malka
ZIBICZA	Rachel
ZIBICZA	Icchak
ZAREMBSKI	Fajwel
ZAREMBSKI	Chela
ZAREMBSKI	Tojba

ZILBERSTEIN	Neta
ZILBERSTEIN	Chawa
ZILBERSTEIN	Liba
ZILBERSTEIN	Sara
ZILBERSTEIN	Beniamin
ZILBERSTEIN	Bluma
ZILBERSTEIN	Malka
ZABOWSKI	Abraham Icchak
ZABOWSKI	Eliahu
ZABOWSKI	Alta
ZIELENIC	Josef
ZIELENIC	Yehudit
ZIELENIC	The children
ZITNER	Abraham
ZITNER	Sara
ZITNER	Yochewet
ZITNER	Jehoszua
ZITNER	Mendel
ZITNER	Szlomo
ZITNER	Tojba Lea
ZITNER	Rachel
ZAREMBER	Abraham
ZAREMBER	Wora
ZAREMBER	Ester
ZAREMBER	Josef

Tet

| TOMKOWICZ | Mosze |
| TOMKOWICZ | Chawa |

TOMKOWICZ	Jakob
TOMKOWICZ	Biniamin (Benje)
TABAK	Szymon Ber
TABAK	Itka
TABAK	Chana
TABAK	Mosze
TENENBOIM	Ester Lea
TENENBOIM	Jakob
TENENBOIM	Dwora
TENENBOIM	Yochewet
TENENBOIM	Becalel
TENENBOIM	Mircza
TENENBOIM	Abraham
TENENBOIM	A son
TENENBOIM	Szlomo
TENENBOIM	Mircza
TENENBOIM	Szymon
TENENBOIM	Henia
TENENBOIM	Nechama
TRESTANOWICZ	Jakob Jehoszua
TRESTANOWICZ	Rajsza
TRESTANOWICZ	Hersz Icchak
TRESTANOWICZ	Malka
TRESTANOWICZ	Fajwel
TRESTANOWICZ	Abraham
TRESTANOWICZ	Batia
TRESTANOWICZ	Cipi
CZOPNIK	Mosze
CZOPNIK	Motka

CZERNA	Rajzel

ʼ

Yud

JAKOBCYNER	Dawid
JAKOBCYNER	Rachel Lea
JAKOBCYNER	Malka
JAKOBCYNER	A daughter
JAKOBCYNER	Henach
JAKOBCYNER	Lea
JAKOBCYNER	Fiszka
JAKOBCYNER	Hinda
JAKOBCYNER	Miriam
JAKOBCYNER	Meir
JAKOBCYNER	Fola
JAKOBCYNER	Chaja
JAKOBCYNER	Welwel
JAKOBCYNER	Fruma
JAKOBCYNER	Sara
JAKOBCYNER	Israel
JAKOBCYNER	Efraim
JARMUZ	Bracha
JARMUZ	Gittel
JOCHELSKI	Alter
JOCHELSKI	Hinda
JOCHELSKI	2 daughters
JOCHELSKI	A son
JASKOLKE	Roszka
JASKOLKE	Nachum
JASKOLKE	Meir

JASKOLKE	Rachel
JELIN	Rachel
JELIN	Cirl
JELIN	Etka
JELIN	Rywka
JANASEK	
JABLONOWICZ	Eliezer Pinchas
JABLONOWICZ	Szajna nee Zilberfenig
JABLONOWICZ	Chaim
JABLONOWICZ	Miriam
JABLONOWICZ	Ester
JABLONOWICZ	Szulamit
JANIEWSKI	Nachum
JANIEWSKI	Henia Rywka
JANIEWSKI	2 children
JANIEWSKI	Welwel
JANIEWSKI	Chaszka
JANIEWSKI	2 children

כ

Kaf

CHMILEWSKI	Jair (Jarke)
CHMILEWSKI	Sara
CHMILEWSKI	Rywka
CHMILEWSKI	Eliezer Pinchas
CHAJKA	Szaul
CHAJKA	The son
CHAJKA	The Daughter
CHARASZCZ	Chaim Icchak
CHARASZCZ	Jenta

CHILER	Rajzel
CHARZANC	Jakob Mosze
CHARZANC	Henia
CHARZANC	Mordechai
CHARZANC	The wife
CHARZANC	The children
CHACHLAWSKI	Icchal
CHACHLAWSKI	Bajla
CHACHLAWSKI	Chilka
CHACHLAWSKI	Lajzer
CHACHLAWSKI	Rasza
CHACHLAWSKI	Bat Szewa
CHACHLAWSKI	Szlomo

ל

Lamed

LITEWKA	Dwora
LITEWKA	Chaim
LITEWKA	Abraham
LITEWKA	Mina
LITEWKA	Kadisz
LITEWKA	Szlomo
LITEWKA	Ettel
LITEWKA	Pinchas
LITEWKA	Dwora
LITEWKA	The son
LITEWKA	Lajb Eli
LEW	Meir
LEW	Chaim
LEW	Alter

LEW	Miriam
LEW	Jehoszua
LEW	Pesza
LEW	Rywka
LEW	Baruch Icchak
LEW	Pesach
LEW	Herszel
LEW	Rachel and a son
LEW	Pesach
LEW	Alta
LEW	Pesach
LEW	Malka
LEW	Reuwen
LEW	The wife
LEW	The children
LEWINSKI	Mosze
LEWINSKI	Roza
LUSTIGMAN	Sima
LEWIN	Mordechai
LEWIN	Raszka
LEWIN	3 children
LITWAK	Jakob
LITWAK	Jochewet
LANDAU	Margalit nee Maradil
LANDAU	Rywka Perl
LANDAU	Rachel Lea
LANDAU	Symcha Bunim
LANDAU	Ester Chaja
LANDAU	Nechama

LANDAU	Szepsl

מ

Mem

MAZOR	Lajb Eli
MAZOR	Malka
MAZOR	Mosze
MAZOR	Ester Chaja
MAZOR	Jakob Szlomo
MAZOR	Szasza
MAZOR	Miriam
MAZOR	Chana
MAZOR	Rywa
MAZOR	Jenta
MAZOR	Icchak
MAZOR	Lajbel
MAZOR	Abraham Ajzik
MADZOWICZ	Cwi (Herszke)
MADZOWICZ	Szosza
MADZOWICZ	Chana
MADZOWICZ	Malka
MADZOWICZ	Chaja
MADZOWICZ	Fradel (Fridka)
MADZOWICZ	Berl
MADZOWICZ	Sana nee Natanel
MADZOWICZ	Rachel
MADZOWICZ	Miriam
MEKER	Alter
MEKER	The wife
MEKER	Sarka

MEKER	Lajzer
MAINCZYK	Sinai
MAINCZYK	Chana
MAINCZYK	The children
MAINCZYK	Mosze
MAINCZYK	Sara
MAINCZYK	The children
MELNIK	Jakob
MELNIK	Rajzel
MELNIK	Chaim
MELNIK	Lea
MELNIK	Bela
MELNIK	Josefa
MAJZNER	Meir
MAJZNER	Raszka
MALBOT	Mosze
MALBOT	The children
MALBOT	Abraham Mosze
MALBOT	Liba
MALBOT	The son
MALBOT	Eliezer
MALBOT	Rachel Endel
MAJNKOT	Sender
MAJNKOT	Rywka
MAJNKOT	Trajna
MAJNKOT	Israel
MAJNKOT	Menachem
MAJNKOT	Welwel
MOSS	Bendet

MOSS	Rachel
MOSS	Zalman
MOSS	Josefa
MOSS	Chawa
MAKOWSKI	Jark
MAKOWSKI	Ester
MAKOWSKI	Pinje
MAKOWSKI	Israelke

נ
Nun

NISNIK	Josefa
NISNIK	Alta
NISNIK	Dworka
NISNIK	Ajzik
NICZEWICZ	Mosze Arie
NICZEWICZ	Alta
NICZEWICZ	Henia Chaja
NICZEWICZ	Szlomo Josef
NICZEWICZ	Henia
NICZEWICZ	Chaim
NICZEWICZ	Herszke
NICZEWICZ	Szoszka
NICZEWICZ	Malka
NICZEWICZ	Frajdl
NICZEWICZ	Chencza

ס
Somach

SLADKI	Jakob
SLADKI	Alta

SLADKI	Rachel
SEGAL	Fiszel
SEGAL	Sara
SEGAL	Jehoszua
SEGAL	Mosze
SEGAL	Liba
SEGAL	Jecheskel
SKAWRANEK	Tuwia
SKAWRANEK	Lea
SKAWRANEK	Raszka
SKAWRANEK	Pesach
SKAWRANEK	Szyfra
SKAWRANEK	Herczke
SKAWRANEK	The wife
SKAWRANEK	The children
SENDAK	Berl Chaczkel
SENDAK	Mjete
SENDAK	The children
SASNE	Zalman
SASNE	Sara
SASNE	The children
SASNE	Mosze
SASNE	Szmuel
SASNE	Gerszon
SASNE	The wife
SASNE	The children
SONJEWICZ	Kalman
SONJEWICZ	Frajdka
SKOCZNADEK	Sara Liba

SALAWICZIK	Fradel
SALAWICZIK	Sara
SOKOLOWICZ	Ginendl
SREBROLOW	Zajdel
SREBROLOW	Perl
SREBROLOW	Tojwa
SREBROLOW	Icchak
SREBROLOW	Mindl
SREBROLOW	Josef
SARNIEWICZ	Zelig
SARNIEWICZ	Ester
SARNIEWICZ	Rywka Lea
SARNIEWICZ	Sara
SARNIEWICZ	Gitl
SARNIEWICZ	Motel
SARNIEWICZ	The wife
SARNIEWICZ	The children
SOKOL	Mosze
SOKOL	Itka
SOKOL	Herszel
SOKOL	Sara Rywka
SOKOL	Ajzik
SOKOL	Meir
SREBROWICZ	Mosze Chaim
SREBROWICZ	Fruma
SREBROWICZ	Dwora
SREBROWICZ	Josef
SREBROWICZ	Chawa
SREBROWICZ	Arie Lajb

SREBROWICZ	Szajna nee Dzisza
SREBROWICZ	Meir
SREBROWICZ	Rasza
SREBROWICZ	Rut

ע
Ayin

EWRIN	Chaja Sara
EDERMAN	Chaja Sara
EDERMAN	Pinchas
EDERMAN	Nechama
EDERMAN	Chaim
EDERMAN	Mendel
EDERMAN	Henia
EDERMAN	Dwora

פ
Peh

PERLMAN	Aharon Jakob, Rabbi
PERLMAN	Rebetzen, the Rabbi's wife
PERLMAN	Chaja Sara
PERLMAN	Chana Basza
PERLMAN	Gitl
PERLMAN	Mosze
PERLMAN	Rywka
FRAJDKES	Szlomo
FRAJDKES	Jakob
PIANKA	J.
FRAKEL	Kusznik
FRAKEL	Szmulik

PACTCZAR	Nachman
PACTCZAR	Malka
PACTCZAR	The grandmother
PIASECKI	Brajndel
PROWOT	
PROWOT	Elka
FRIDMAN	Sara
FRIDMAN	Lajbel
FRIDMAN	Dwora
FRIDMAN	Gerszon
FIERTAG	Gitl
FIERTAG	Sara
FIERTAG	Ruth
PTASZEWICZ	Chaim
PTASZEWICZ	Doba
PTASZEWICZ	Lea
PTASZEWICZ	Ben Cion
PTASZEWICZ	Tewl
PTASZEWICZ	Fajga
PTASZEWICZ	Arie
PTAK	Yehuda
PTAK	Lea
PTAK	Lajbel
PTAK	Rajzel
FAJGENBLUM	Aszer
FAJGENBLUM	Szewa
PASTERNAK	Aba
PASTERNAK	The wife
PASTERNAK	The Daughter

PIEKAR	Wolf
PIEKAR	The wife
PIEKAR	The children
PIEKAR	Mordechai
PIEKAR	Jenta Chaja
PIEKAR	Welwel
PIEKAR	Chana Basza
PIEKAR	Aharon Hersz
PIEKAR	Chawa
PIEKAR	Dyna
PIEKAR	Israel
PIEKAR	Chaim
PIEKAR	Rywka
PIEKAR	Szlomo
PIEKAR	Gitl
PIEKAR	Baruch
PIEKAR	Fajga
PIEKAR	Noach
FLISZKA	Herszel
FLISZKA	Fajga
FLISZKA	Meir
FLISZKA	Bajla
FLISZKA	Batia
FLISZKA	Israel
FLISZKA	Sara
FLISZKA	Icchak
FLISZKA	Malka

Tzadik

CZICZOWICZ	Szaul
CZICZOWICZ	Ester
CZICZOWICZ	Aharon Szlomo
CZICZOWICZ	Szlomo
CZICZOWICZ	Awiezer
CZICZOWICZ	Josefa
CZICZOWICZ	Rachel
CZICZOWICZ	Sara
CZICZOWICZ	Chawa Lea
CZICZOWICZ	Sara
CZICZOWICZ	Szmulka
CZICZOWICZ	Noami
CZIRANKA	Rachel

ק

Kof

CUKIERCWAJG	Berisz
CUKIERCWAJG	The children
CZEDERBAUM	Julesz
CZEDERBAUM	Zine nee Majzner
CUKIEROWICZ	Reuwen
CUKIEROWICZ	Pesza
KIWEJKA	Szlomo
KIWEJKA	Alta
KIWEJKA	Lajb
KIWEJKA	Rajzel
KIWEJKA	Chawa
KIWEJKA	Ester
KIWEJKA	Josefa
KIWEJKA	Mosze Hersz

KIWEJKA	Alta (Chaja Rywka)
KIWEJKA	Miriam
KIWEJKA	Abcze
KIWEJKA	Lea
KIWEJKA	Fajgel
KIWEJKA	Szajka (Jeszayahu)
KIWEJKA	Mordechai
KIWEJKA	Chasia
KIWEJKA	Chana
KRUPINSKI	Szmuel
KRUPINSKI	Itka Lea
KRUPINSKI	Natan
KRUPINSKI	Fruma
KRUPINSKI	Szabtai
KRUPINSKI	Szlomo
KRUPINSKI	Ester Malka
KRUPINSKI	Dwora
KRUPINSKI	Menucha
KRUPINSKI	Zalman
KRUPINSKI	Akiwa
KRUPINSKI	Bina
KRUPINSKI	Abraham Berl
KRUPINSKI	Szajnka
KRUPINSKI	Icze
KRUPINSKI	Kalman
KRUPINSKI	Miriam
KRUPINSKI	Eliahu
KRUPINSKI	Cwi

KRUPINSKI	Chana
KRUPINSKI	Liba
KASCZEWKI	Abraham Icchak
KASCZEWKI	Malka
KASCZEWKI	Bajla
KASCZEWKI	Chaja
KOCIAK	Zalman
KOCIAK	Chaja
KOCIAK	Lea
KOCIAK	Fajgel
KOCIAK	Lajbel
KOCIAK	Malka
KOCIAK	Kjakob
KASCZEWKI	Chaim Michael
KASCZEWKI	Alta
KASCZEWKI	Szifra
KASCZEWKI	Chaja Lea
KASCZEWKI	Fajwel
KASCZEWKI	Abraham Icchak
KASCZEWKI	Jehudit'ke
KASCZEWKI	Lajbel
KASCZEWKI	Dwoszka
KASCZEWKI	Michla
KAPLAN	Kalman
KAPLAN	Mosze
KAPLAN	Frajdel
KAPLAN	Ben Cion
KAPLAN	Jakob
KAPLAN	Chaja

KAPLAN	Sonia
KAPLAN	Rachel
KAPLAN	Awiezer
KAPLAN	Nachman
KAPLAN	Jeszayahu
KAPLAN	Ita
KANOWICZ	Sara Brajna
KANOWICZ	The Daughter
KANOWICZ	Icze Lajb
KANOWICZ	The wife
KANOWICZ	The children
KANOWICZ	Akiwa
KANOWICZ	The wife
KANOWICZ	The children
KAWIAR	Ozer
KAWIAR	Chana
KAWIAR	The children
KRAWAT	Herszel
KRAWAT	Motel
KRAWAT	The son
KOWADLO	Eliezer
KOWADLO	Frajda
KAWKE	Jakob
KAWKE	Ester Rywka
KAWKE	Rachel
KAWKE	Sara
KROLEWSKI	Chaim Welwel
KROLEWSKI	Peszka
KROLEWSKI	Frajdl

KROLEWSKI	Doba
KROLEWSKI	Eli Dawid
KOPITOWSKI	Mosze Aharon
KOPITOWSKI	Abraham Meir
KOPITOWSKI	Chana
KOPITOWSKI	Szmuel Dawid
KOPITOWSKI	The wife
KOPITOWSKI	3 children
KROSNOWORSKI	Szmuel
KROSNOWORSKI	Ester
KROSNOWORSKI	Nachman
KON	Michael
KON	Cwia
KON	Abraham
KON	Sara'ke
KON	Etcze
KON	Szajna
KON	The children
KON	Jakob
KON	Doba
KON	Rajchl
KON	Herszel
KON	Motel
KON	Cirl
KROWCZYK	Frajdl
KROWCZYK	Lewi
KROWCZYK	Rachel
KROWCZYK	The children
KROWCZYK	Jakob

KROWCZYK	Ester Rywka
KROWCZYK	Abraham Berl
KROWCZYK	Rachel
KROWCZYK	Sara
KIEK	Zalman
KIEK	Basza
KIEK	Chaja and a child

ר

Raish

RUBINSZTEIN	Miriam
RUBINSZTEIN	Hinda
RUBINSZTEIN	Icchak
RUBINSZTEIN	2 daughters
RADZYLEWSKI	Fajwel
RADZYLEWSKI	Cirl
RADZYLEWSKI	The children
RACKI	Jakob
RACKI	Gitl
RACKI	Iser
RACKI	Fajgele
RACKI	Szmuel
RACKI	Rywka
RACKI	Reuwen
RACKI	Iser
RACKI	Malka
RACKI	Miriam
RYC	Chaszka
RYC	2 children
RAJGROCKI	Pinchas

RAJGROCKI	Itka
RAJGROCKI	Symcha
RAJGROCKI	Pesach
ROTKOWSKI	Abraham
ROTKOWSKI	The wife
ROTKOWSKI	The children
ROTKOWSKI	Edzia
ROTKOWSKI	Jente
ROTKOWSKI	Sara
ROTKOWSKI	Yehuda
ROTKOWSKI	Icchak
RAWICZ	Welwel
RAWICZ	Chana
RAWICZ	Cila Doba
ROZENBERG	Szmuel Jakob
ROZENBERG	The wife
ROZENBERG	Lajbel
ROZENBERG	The wife
ROZENBERG	The children

ש

Sheen

SZCZINAGEL	Michael
SZCZINAGEL	Abraham Lajzer
SZCZINAGEL	Sara Gitl
SZCZINAGEL	Henia Rywka
SZCZINAGEL	Cwia
SZCZINAGEL	Golda
SZCZINAGEL	Rachel
SZCZINAGEL	Josef

SZCZINAGEL	Fajga
SZCZINAGEL	Chaja
SZKLA	Jechiel
SZKLA	Chana
SZKLA	Brajndel
SZKLA	Rywka
SZKLA	Gitl
SZKLA	Golda
SZKLA	Baruch
SZKLA	Lajcza
SZKLA	Ester
SZKLA	Szajnka
SZKLA	Bat Szewa
SZKLA	Bela Itka
SZKLA	Bendet
SZKLA	Elka
SZKLA	Chai
SZKLA	Szajka
SZKLA	Itka
SZKLA	Eli
SZOPSZYK	Chaja Sara
SZOPSZYK	Malka
SZTERN	Efraim
SZTERN	Szajna
SZTERN	The children
SZLEPOWICZ	Berl Lajb
SZLEPOWICZ	Sonia
SZLEPOWICZ	Mosze
SZEWKES	Chaja Sara

SZWARC	Lea
SZWARC	Dwora
SZIF	Josef
SZERSZEWICZ	Nachman
SZERSZEWICZ	Bendet
SZERSZEWICZ	Fajga
SZERSZEWICZ	The children
SZERENIEC	Mindl
SZERENIEC	Chaja Ita

[Pages 267-269]

Jablonka

Surname	Name
BIEWICZ	Fyszel
BIEWICZ	Fajga Fola
BIEWICZ	Dow
GRUSZKA	Mosze Icchak
GRUSZKA	Szmuel
GRUSZKA	Sara Rajzel
DOMBEK	Lajbel
DOMBEK	Rywka
DOMBEK	Drezl
WAJSBORD	Abraham Dow
WAJSBORD	Miriam Lea
WAJSBORD	Pesach
WAJSBORD	Chana
WAJSBORD	Gdalyahu
WAJSBORD	Szmuel
WAJSBORD	Rywka
WAJSBORD	Szoszana
WAJSBORD	Cypora
WAJSBORD	Mendl
WAJSBORD	Rachel
WAJSBORD	Moszke
WAJSBORD	Mendl Mosze
WAJSBORD	Szajna Cirl
WAJSBORD	Mendl
WIERZSZWA	Majszka
WIERZSZWA	Sara Lea

WIERZSZWA	Lajbel
WIERZSZWA	Zisl
ZISZIWCZA	Eliahu
ZISZIWCZA	Gutka
ZISZIWCZA	Michal
ZISZIWCZA	Mosze Lajbel
ZISZIWCZA	Rachel
ZISZIWCZA	Fajgel
ZISZIWCZA	Szajna Cyrel
ZISZIWCZA	Rywka
TOPOR	Aszer
TOPOR	Eltka
TOPOR	The children
LEW	Sender
LEW	Alta
LEW	Bluma
LEW	Majka
NAGORNA	Icze
NAGORNA	Malcza
NAGORNA	The children
SEGAL	Liba
SEGAL	Jecheskel
SEGAL	Nachman
SEGAL	Sara
SEGAL	The children
SEGAL	Mordechai
SEGAL	Kajla
SEGAL	Rachel
SEGAL	Mosze Lajbel

SEGAL	Zeltka
SEGAL	Motel
SEGAL	Nachman
SEGAL	Rajzel
SEGAL	Ester
SEGAL	Chaim
SEGAL	Sulka
SEGAL	Sara Rajzel
SEGAL	Hitka
SOKOL	Rywka
SOKOL	Mosze Chaim
SOKOL	Icze
SOKOL	Menachel
SOKOL	Rajza Basza
SOKOL	Szmule
SOKOL	Frajdka
SREWEROLOW	Motel
SREWEROLOW	Zalman
SREWEROLOW	Rywka
SREWEROLOW	Meir Lajb
SREWEROLOW	Raszka
SREWEROLOW	Jona
SREWEROLOW	Chana
SREWEROLOW	Meir Lajbel
FRAJDMUTER	Josef
FRAJDMUTER	Itka
FRAJDMUTER	Benjamin
FRAJDMUTER	Chaja
FRAJDMUTER	Dwora

PIANKA	Mosze
PIANKA	Sara Bajla
PIANKA	Abraham
PIANKA	Chaja
KACZEWKA	Chaim
KACZEWKA	Bluma
KACZEWKA	Dworka
KLASEWICZ	Jakob
KLASEWICZ	Riszka
KLASEWICZ	Icchak
KLASEWICZ	Dawid
KOZSZAL	Lajbel
KOZSZAL	Chana
KOZSZAL	The children
KOZSZAL	Kadisz
KOZSZAL	Jaspa
KOZSZAL	The children
KOWALINSKI	Szmuel
KOWALINSKI	Sara
KOWALINSKI	Baruch
KOWALINSKI	Abrahame'le
KOWALINSKI	Meir
KOWALINSKI	Szarcia
KOWALINSKI	Icchal
KOWALINSKI	Baruch

A wedding in the shtetl

The English Part

Visoka-Mozovietsk – Wysokie Mazowiecki

From Its Beginning to the End of the 19th Century

Visoka Mozovietsk, near the Bruce River, is located seven kilometers from the Shepitova station of the Bialystok-Warsaw line. It is considered one of the oldest settlements in the Mezovia region of Poland, and is mentioned as such as early as the first half of the 13th century (1239).

There is no information on the beginnings of a Jewish settlement "Arba Aratzot" Council in connection with the taxes it was obliged to pay. A document from the year 1752 has been preserved, which is directly concerned with the Visoka Mozovietsk Jewish community. It describes a dispute over the membership of that community, between Tchecbanovitsi and Vengrov, each of them the head of an "area". The quarrel had to do with the right of jurisdiction over the little town. The dispute was brought before the "Arba Aratzot" Council and the judges, Rabbi Yehoshua Levi and Rabbi Berish Segal of Cracow, in the presence of representatives from Tchechanovitsi and Vengrov. Since neither of the two sides could prove the justice of its case, the judges decided that the Visoka Mozovietsk community should belong to neither of them. And, indeed, from then on Visoka Mozovietsk has been an independent community.

One hundred and fifty years later, in the second half of the 19th century, there were 600 Jewish households in Visoka Mozovietsk.

From the Beginning of 20th Century to the End of World War I

The Jewish population of Visoka Mozovietsk was composed, more or less, of three economic classes:

1) Merchants, mainly shopkeepers;
2) Craftsmen;
3) Workers, mainly apprentices of the craftsmen who hoped to become craftsmen in their turn.

* * *

In 1905, the first Russian revolution broke out, but it passed over without leaving any visible effects on the little town, frozen in its old patterns, whose way of life continued as though nothing had happened. But at about the same time, an event took place in Visoka which rocked the inhabitants of the town, Christians and Jews alike, and was to remain etched in their memories for years to come.

This extraordinary event was the famous robbery of the Russian Government Bank, the Kaznochestvo, by members of the Polish Socialist Party (P.P.S.) which was headed by Joseph Pilsudski.

The daring robbery, successfully organized and carried out, made a strong impression on Poland in particular, and on other parts of the Russian Empire as well. And the strongest impression of all was upon the residents of the town who were eyewitnesses to the bold and violent deed.

* * *

As in most of the towns of Poland and Lithuania, Jewish life in Visoka Mozovietsk centered around two points:
1) Making a living; and
2) the religious way of life, observed zealously and meticulously.

Contact with the world outside the town was limited to trips made by merchants to the big cities, Bialystok and Warsaw, to buy merchandise, and to the district capital, Lamzja, where the government institutions were centered. In addition, the Hassidim might make a journey to the "rebbes", and the young people, yearning to study Torah, went to Lomzja or to big yeshivas in Lithuania.

Visoka was fortunate in never having been burned down in any conflagration, despite the fact that most of its buildings were of wood. In most of the neighboring villages, fires would break out from time to time, burning large areas to the ground. The old rabbi, the Zaddik, claimed that according to a legend, their town was blessed so that fire could not devour it.

* * *

At the end of the first decade of the present century, and the beginning of the second decade, the Polish nationalist extremists proclaimed a boycott of Jewish places of business. For some reason, it was the fate of Visoka to be one of the first fronts in the war of the anti-Semitic nationalists against Jewish merchants. The local priest was at the head of the wild incitement to a pogrom. This anti-Semitic outbreak was accompanied by acts of violence against the Jews and even murder.

* * *

The years of World War I passed in Visoka without any great shocks. Nevertheless, basic changes did occur, which were to leave their mark on the development of the town in the coming years. Right at the beginning of the war, the town was captured by the Germans who occupied it until the war ended. The Germans, under the rule of Kaiser Wilhelm II, did not molest the Jewish population; on the contrary, they granted the Jews rights they had never had under the Tsars. Shortly after the town was captured, the military government was exchanged for civil rule The German civil authorities, middle-aged people, evinced a liberal attitude to the Jews and even befriended Jewish families with whom they maintained close contacts.

It is noteworthy that under the German occupation, public and cultural activities among the Jewish population started to flourish. Activities which had been forbidden under the Russians, at least officially, Zionist societies and secular cultural activities which had been very limited under the Tsars, were now permitted. The younger generation, thirsty for enlightenment, came out in the open and began to develop all kinds of cultural and public activities.

As soon as the ban on Zionist activity was lifted, Zionist organizations started to circulate the idea of a national movement among the young people and other in the Jewish population. The first Zionist society was a branch of the "Tzeirey-Zion". Shortly thereafter, a branch of "Poalei Zion" was established, active mainly among working youth. It spread the ideas of socialistic Zionism, including "hachshara" (preparatory training) and "aliya" (immigration to Eretz Israel).

In the same period, the Maccabi sports organization was established in Visoka. Its first head was a German army man named Meichsner, then serving under the civil authority of the conquering army.

One of the most important cultural activities during this period was the establishment of a public library. For the culture-starved youth it opened a window to the wide world of Hebrew and Yiddish literature, as well as to a wide range of world literature in translation into those two languages. The library also invited outside lecturers and writers to appear, and organized discussion evenings on various literary subjects, with the local people taking part.

Under the German occupation a vital change took place in the field of education as well. No longer was the traditional "heder" the ruling force of the Jewish population; alongside it, modern and progressive educational institutions took their place.

Between the Two World Wars

The Economic Situation

The establishment of the autonomous Polish Republic began badly for the three million Jews within its borders. The newly independent Poles celebrated their new authority with pogroms and riots against the Jews.

The Jewish community of Visoka Mozovietsk received its share of the pogroms (in August 1920). The Jewish representatives to the Polish "Saym" (the Polish parliament) protested to the government and demanded the punishment of the rioters.

* * *

As in all Polish towns, the economy of the Jewish population of Visoka was based on trade and on crafts. The Jews bought the agricultural produce from the peasants in the neighborhood and sold them manufactured products and hand-made products in their turn.

However, relations with the Gentile population were not particularly friendly. Despite the fact that they had close trade relations, with most of the agricultural products being sold to the Jews, while Jewish merchants and craftsmen supplied the peasants with clothing, shoes, kitchen utensils, work implements and tools, and other goods - a mountain of alienation was rising between the two sectors of the population.

An independent Poland established an extremist, nationalistic and anti-Semitic line from the very start, which expressed itself, among other things, in pushing the Jews out of their economic position. The older generation somehow or other adjusted itself to the new reality of a difficult struggle for its daily existence. Jewish youth, however, found itself before a blank wall in the face of the desperate economic situation he acutely anti-Jewish policy taken by the Polish government entire twenty years of the existence of an autonomous Polish nation.

The situation became worse in the 1930's reaching the point where a large portion of the Jewish population was able to survive only thanks to the regular assistance it received from relatives in America.

As a consequence of the hard struggle to make a living, the Jews gradually became aware that things would be easier, if they established n financial their own financial projects based on mutual help. The result was the founding of a cooperative bank, whose participants included both merchants and craftsmen. After a while, however, the merchants split off from the cooperative bank and established a bank of their own. From then on, there were two credit institutions operating in Visoka.

As in all the Eastern European cities and towns, the traditional charitable organizations operated in Visoka, as well as the more modern philanthropic institutions.

Zionist Youth Movements

Zionist youth movements that reached their peak in Eastern n the 1920's and 1930's served as a great stimulus to the development and advancement of the youth of Visoka. In 1927, a branch of "Hashomer Haleumi" was set up; this afterwards became "Hanoar Hazioni", the biggest youth movement in the town. Many of its members studied Hebrew, gave lectures on Zionist subjects, and did practical Zionist work, mainly for the Keren Kayemet (Jewish National Fund). In later years, a "Betar" movement was set up, founded by the Revisionist party.

But the main purpose of the pioneering movements, and to some extent of the Zionist parties as well, was "aliya" - immigration to Israel - and the preparation for it ("hachshara"). Actually, immigration to Israel had begun as early as 1919-1920, though on an individual basis.

In the 1920's and 1930's, the "Hechalutz" organization was founded in Visoka. Its most important project was the establishment of a "hachshara" (training farm) which afterwards became the training center for the entire vicinity.

* * *

Visoka was almost entirely a zionistic town. The tone of public life was set by the Zionist Parties, the most prominent of which were: Pole Zion, Zeirei-Zion, the General Zionists, Mizrachi, and the Revisionist Movement.

Visoka on the Eve of the Holocaust

The political and economic situation of the Jews of Poland deteriorated. Visoka was one of the towns which suffered a pogrom in 1937. Jewish property was looted or destroyed, many Jewish houses were damaged, and 23 persons were injured.

There were Jews who lived under the illusion that the bad situation was a passing thing, a temporary ill wind. But in fact, this phenomenon had deep roots in the total Jewish-Polish situation, a fact that became evident in the years just preceding World War II. Changes in attitude turned up in the market place, in the Polish shops, and in other places. It reached a point where the Jews had the feeling that the Poles were complaining about them living in the town, of their supporting them-selves, of their very existence. It was hard for a Jew of Visoka to accept the new reality, although for a long time it had been possible to sense the approaching storm.

The Holocaust

At the outbreak of World War II, there were five hundred Jewish families, comprising about 2500 souls, in Visoka Mozovietsk. On September 10th, 1939, the town was captured by the Germans, who set it on fire.

On September 12th, all the Jewish men were herded into the church, where they were kept for three days without food or water. At the end of that time, they were sent to Zembrov. On the way to Zembrov, the weak and weary were shot.

On September 19th, an order was given that by 3 P.M. on the next day, all the Jews of Visoka must be out of town. All the Jews became panic-stricken, because they didn't know where to run to. They ran off with nothing but the clothes on their backs. With the exception of the men who had been taken away earlier, the Jews of Visoka went to the neighboring town and to Bialystok.

On September 26th, 1939, in accordance with the Molotov-Ribbentrop agreement, the Germans withdrew from the eastern regions of Poland, and Visoka passed to Soviet authority. The people who had been expelled from Visoka could now return to their homes, and even those Jews who had been transported to Germany came back.

With the help of the Soviet authorities, the Jewish returnees reconstructed their burned town. It didn't take long, and Visoka again had a Jewish population of 1,100.

On July 24th, 1941, two days after the outbreak of the German-Russian War, the Germans recaptured Visoka. On the very same day, the murderous Nazi regime began its activities. On August 15th, the "Judenrat" received an order that on the next morning, all the Jews must assemble in the marketplace. Everyone was gripped by panic. From information reaching them from other places, they could guess the significance of this gathering. A large portion of the Jewish population ran away from the town.

On August 16th, at the given hour, all the Jews still left in Visoka gathered in the marketplace. For a whole day and night, the weary, resigned people waited there. Only the following day at 7 A.M. did they receive a notification that due to transportation difficulties, the committee was unable to arrive. It was found out afterwards that the real reason the committee didn't come was because it was busy with the expulsion of Jews from other towns.

This first "Action", plus reports from other places that life was more secure in the ghettoes, influenced the heads of the Jewish community to request the authorities to set up a ghetto in Visoka, mainly for fear of pogroms on the part of the local Gentiles. They achieved their ghetto after a great deal of maneuvering.

On November 23rd, 1941, Jews from the neighboring communities in Yablonka, Kulish, Vitong, Dombrova and other places, were sent to the ghetto in Visoka. These Jews, 20,000 people in all, were pushed into the three streets of the ghetto, which were surrounded by barbed wire.

The "Judenrat" (Jewish Community Council) consisted of thirteen members: Alter Zack, Chairman; Avraham Hertz, Fishel Segal; Meir Meisner; Bezalel Tannenbaum; Hirsch-Yitzhak Trostonovitz; David Mazur; Eliahu Vunsover; Bernholtz; Pessah Skobronek; Ya'acov Melnick; Shmuel Isaac Yellin; Tankum Mekulish; and Hava Yellin who served as secretary. Alter Zack and Avraham Hertz were the ghetto representatives to the German authorities.

What did the Jews live from in the ghetto? The oil presses were opened, one by Isaac Kraponsky, and the other by Ephraim Stern, the shoemaker.

The "Judenrat" had to supply workers to the Germans. The first task was to spread sand on the roads. Some of the younger people worked for the "Pritzim" – the big estate owners. Their wages – potatoes and other agricultural products – were passed on to the "Judenrat" which divided the products among all of the Jewish population.

The "Judenrat" organized a soup kitchen, and all the needy, primarily those who had come from the nearby settlements, received a hot meal twice a day. The "Judenrat" and the Jewish police force organized the work in such a way that they were also able to supply food to the Jews from nearby towns, who worked at road-building on the Bialystok - Warsaw and Tiktin road. Although it was very dangerous, they exposed themselves to great risks in order to help others in distress.

With the onset of winter, the Germans sent the young Jewish people to the woods to chop down trees, to cut them into logs and to bring them to the Germans as firewood for heating purposes. As payment for the work, the Jews were permitted to dig up the tree roots for their own use. These roots were passed to the "Judenrat" which divided them as fairly as possible among the inhabitants of the ghetto, to be used for heating and cooking.

The work to which they were sent by the Germans - breaking stones and paving roads – was done as forced labor, and without payment. Food for the workers was supplied by the "Judenrat". Skilled craftsmen and others, who still supported themselves from their own work, would pay an indemnity to the "Judenrat" instead of doing the forced labor. And, as already mentioned, the workers of the agricultural estates gave the food products they received to the "Judenrat", which divided it as best they could. This all made it easier for the "Judenrat" to fulfill its functions. This is the situation that existed until the ghetto was liquidated. The old, the poor and the solitary lived in the fire department building, and existed from the charity fund of the community. The "Judenrat" did its best to keep concentration of large groups of people in any one place to a minimum and arranged for some of the single people to be placed in various homes.

Much courage was shown, and many people put their own lives in danger in the ghetto. Especially noteworthy were Alter Zack, the chairman of the "Judenrat" and his daughter, Dr. Golda Zack. Dr. Golda Zack worked day and night to care for the sick and feeble, receiving no payment whatsoever. She worked over and above her strength, even in the coldest winter nights. As for Alter Zack, he risked his life more than once by standing up to the Germans in order to defend the Jews. Once, when there was an alarm and most of the people ran for their lives, Alter Zack and his son, Yudel, were left all alone in the ghetto. For some reason, the Germans shut their eyes to his impertinence, and didn't punish him, possibly because they had orders not to harm the head of the "Judenrat" in order to prevent unrest among the Jewish population. According to plan, the Jews were to be done away with by stages, and the time had not yet come to get rid of the head of this Jewish community.

On Sunday, November 1ˢᵗ, 1942, some 300 wagons reached Visoka. The Germans explained that the wagons hat been brought for the purpose of transferring saplings for forest planting. It all sounded very suspicious, and some of the residents of the ghetto ran off to the woods the very same evening.

Early on Monday morning, the Jews were ordered out to the marketplace. At that time, the young people were doing roadwork outside the ghetto. The Germans didn't allow the Jews to take anything at all with them, and ordered everyone onto the wagons. The sound of their weeping and their cries must have reached heaven itself. The young people, as mentioned above, were working outside the ghetto on that day and didn't know what was going on there. Suddenly, the German work supervisor appeared and within a few minutes, hundreds of German soldiers arrived on the spot. Hordes of Gentiles turned up too, armed with axes and pitchforks, and waiting for spoils. The Germans ordered the workers onto trucks; not one of them could escape.

At this point, the part played by the local Poles in exterminating the Jewish population should be noted. At times, their cruelty and hatred towards the Jews exceeded that of the Germans. At the same time, one must recall those few saintly individuals who endangered their own lives and hid Jews in secret hiding places on their property and in their yards. Their deeds are none the less praiseworthy, despite the fact that they were well paid in gold, silver and precious stones. The people deported from the ghetto were brought to the camp in Zembrov, where 17,500 Jews were concentrated. Conditions in the camp were very difficult. The food rations per day, for twelve people, consisted of one loaf of bread weighing about two pounds, and made of bran and chestnut flour. Each person also received half a liter (quart) of a watery, unsalted soup made of rotten potatoes. The death rate in the Zembrov camp reached one hundred persons a day. It was mainly the children and the old people who died.

On January 15ᵗʰ, 1943, the Germans started to evacuate the Zembrov camp. They claimed that the people were being sent off to work. All the sick people in the local hospital were taken off to the Christian cemetery and were murdered there together.

As for the others, those who could still stand on their own legs, were taken out at night, group by group, and brought to the train station of Chizev on trailers. They were forced onto the trailers in a cruel fashion: they ran under a barrage of blows. By the time they arrived at the train station, many of them froze.

On January 17ᵗʰ, 1943, the 11ᵗʰ of Shvat, 5703, they reached Auschwitz. According to practice, at that extermination camp, the old, the women and children were separated from the younger men. The first group was taken off to the gas chambers right away, while the men who could still be used for work were placed into a blockade work camp.

In general, young women from other cities were also taken off for work details. The women of Visoka had no such luck, not even the young ones. They were sentenced to death in the gas chambers as soon as they reached the infamous extermination camp. Only two young girls from Visoka who were in Auschwitz survived – the Golobradka sisters – because they happened to have been brought from the Pruzjina ghetto.

Rabbi Abraham Jacob Pearlman was the last rabbi of the Visoka Mozovietsk community. Rabbi Pearlman was not only an exceptionally learned man, he was also known for his wisdom, his exceptional personality, his fine manners. During the forty years that he was rabbi of Visoka, he fulfilled his post as spiritual leader of the community with devotion and success. He was known throughout the whole area, and people from neighboring towns turned to him with questions on "halacha" (religious practice) and asked his advice on worldly matters as well.

Rabbi Pearlman remained the shepherd of his flock in the dark days, when infliction rained down upon his followers. He was with them in the Visoka ghetto, in the Zembrov ghetto, and he went to his tragic end in Auschwitz together with the thousands of other Jews from Visoka, who were murdered in the gas chambers by the Nazis. May their names be erased.

* * *

We shall light a memorial candle to the last chapter in the history of Jewish Visoka, the frightful chapter of the ghetto, in whose confines the Jews were caged in a never-ending nightmare. One wondrous light shone through it all: In the sharing of this insufferable fate which befell the sanctified community of Visoka, in its final days, great acts of personal courage were performed, and devotion and love of Israel of the highest quality were called into being.

The cup of tears overflows... the wound is open and does not heal. One seeks the tiniest sign of comfort, and the heart longs for the retribution of God.

May the names of our holy ones be glorified and sanctified forever.
God will take retribution.

Talmud Torah 1934

NAME INDEX